OUR LAST
innocent
MOMENT

JULIE PONESSE, PHD

Our Last Innocent Moment
Julie Ponesse

Brownstone Institute • Austin, Texas

Copyright © 2024 Brownstone Institute, (Austin, Texas)
Creative Commons Attribution International 4.0

Physical ISBN 9781630692582
Digital ISBN 9781630692575

Design: Vanessa Mendozzi

OUR LAST
innocent
MOMENT

JULIE PONESSE, PHD

BROWNSTONE
INSTITUTE

For those we could not save,
and those who were saved in the trying

Contents

I speak of
unpopular facts.

—Hannah Arendt, *The Jewish Writings*

Acknowledgements

It is hardly surprising that some of the greatest creative human endeavours — in literature, art, science, music, even architecture — owe their existence as much to negative forces as to positive ones. Necessity is the mother of invention they say, but so too are instability, terror, apathy, chaos, and betrayal.

In many ways, it was the actions of the worst of us over the last four years that made this book possible...and necessary. I owe a debt of gratitude to these people. And where there is a debt, it ought to be paid. For that reason, I want to thank (but not to bestow the honour of naming) every political leader who ruled without wisdom, every doctor and nurse who complied without critical thought, every judge who rested on the laurels of judicial notice, and every citizen who betrayed the bonds of family, friendship, and civic duty.

Less facetiously, I am grateful to those who resisted all of these.

Thank you, first and foremost, to Brownstone Institute founder, Jeffrey Tucker, who wrote one day with a link to the institute's fellowship page asking "Interested in this?" Without Brownstone and an anonymous donor I likely wouldn't have written this book. When you are engaged in a creative enterprise, you need not just practical support but support of the spirit — intellectual bucking-up from those who believe that the world needs what you are making. There is none better at this than Jeffrey Tucker. Jeff, why aren't you publishing all the world's books?

To Beth (who, of course, isn't really Beth), whose story and feelings I hope I have done justice. To Kelly-Sue Oberle and everyone at the citizen's and national inquiries who dared to share their stories when they were repeatedly told they don't matter, and to Sean Hartman and the lost others, who never had the chance to do so.

To the many intellectuals who continue to think and write and converse in our deep culture of silence, and to Heather Heying, in particular, who graciously shared her thoughts on certainty and audacity.

To a perpetually anonymous confidant, idea-'finesser,' and sculptor of narrative, who understands more than most that the act of remembering is an act of humanity.

To my family, my daughter in particular, who makes everything worthwhile and who knows that "Mommy is writing a book" but who wishes, instead, that I had more time for tower-building and ladybug-hunting with no timelines. (I'm done, sweetheart – let the building and hunting commence!)

And, finally, to everyone who was told to sit down, shut up, and just get along…and who stood up and spoke out anyway, thank you, THANK YOU! You are tired, I know, but you are making a bigger impression than you will ever know.

Introduction

We had best look our times and lands searchingly in the face, like a physician diagnosing some deep disease.

— Walt Whitman, *Democratic Vistas*

D o you remember where you were when it happened? Who you were with?

That moment when you first felt the ground shift beneath you. When your friends seemed a little less familiar, family a little more distant.

When your trust in our highest institutions — government, medicine, law, journalism —started to unravel.

The last time your naive optimism allowed you to believe that the world is, generally, as it seems.

Our last innocent moment.

o o o

If you are reading this, then there is a good chance you have your own last moment of innocence, even if the details of it are a little hazy. Sometime in 2020, there was a fundamental shift in how many of us view the world. The delicate network of core beliefs about what makes it possible to navigate life with some measure of stability and reliability — that medicine is a patient-focused institution, that journalists pursue truth, that the courts track

justice, that our friends would behave in certain predictable ways
— started to unravel.

There was a paradigm shift in how we live and relate to each
other. A shift in attitude. A shift in trust. A shift away from a
world we can never revisit, an innocence we can never recover.
The before times and the after times. And, though we didn't know
it then, there would be certain unrecoverable changes to life from
which we are still reeling.

Now, an almost unfathomable four years after the World Health
Organization declared COVID-19 a global pandemic, our once
seemingly stable world is unrecognizable. Medicine and science
have proven themselves to be closed systems, echo chambers
in which even the most minute deviation from their orthodoxies cannot survive. Journalism is now a powerful narrative spin
machine. Our courts are show trials that employ predetermined
conclusions as matters of professional practice, and even our most
promising politicians seem to undergo a mystical transformation
to silence and conformity once admitted to office.

We have, in general, become untethered from a world that
seemed to be spinning with a certain cadence, from the relationships that framed our days and our futures, and maybe even from
who we were as individuals. We have set ourselves adrift from
life framed by core Western liberal values — liberty, equality, and
autonomy, most fundamentally — and we find ourselves broken
and unrecognizable without them. And, most treacherously, we
seem to be tinkering with the fundamental principles of civility:
toleration, patience, respect, and kindness.

Even now, each day brings yet another set of unfathomable
revelations. We learned that calls for emergency medical services
decreased in 2020 and then spiked in 2022, contradicting the
narrative that COVID-19 killed unprecedented numbers of people
and that the COVID-19 shots are perfectly "safe and effective."[1]
We learned that the Chief Justice of the Supreme Court co-chaired
a committee on COVID-19 with the federal Minister of Justice

since 2020. And Sheila Lewis, the transplant patient removed from a transplant list because of her vaccination status, died on the day the Liberal government posted on Twitter "Every Canadian deserves access to the health care they need, when they need it." *Every* Canadian?

Our world has become a house of mirrors, a patchwork of shattered layers of institutions and narratives and individuals that have shown themselves to be illogical and capricious, and yet somehow capable of invading the most intimate corners of our lives. We face a health care crisis, an economic crisis, a housing crisis, a food crisis, and a land crisis. Our children are losing their childhoods and, with it, their innocence. Families are imploding. The world is burning, literally and metaphorically.

We find ourselves in a hellish reality that the Freedom Convoy made poignant to us. Canada no longer feels like home. It is no longer a safe haven. Parents are struggling to feed their families, to educate their children, to navigate a crumbling health care system. Neighbours feel like strangers. Friend groups are torn apart. Our flag waves weakly and "Best country in the world" is now an empty phrase.

And, on top of all of this, we face a deep constitutional crisis, not in the technical sense — though I think our Canadian constitution has proven itself to be useful only to the degree that it is in capable hands — but a crisis of who we are as a people, what we are made of, what *constitutes* us in a very literal sense.

Looking back, there were no clear signs, no cautionary tales, no warnings from friends that could have prepared us for what was to come. There have always been corporations that couldn't be trusted, collective missteps, and historical atrocities, but we were making progress, weren't we? Hadn't we learned from the past? Weren't we becoming a little more enlightened? A little more tolerant and patient? Weren't our institutions, for the most part, getting us somewhere, or a sign that we had gotten somewhere?

Before 2020, our relationships were framed by probabilities, by predictions about what and who we could rely on in times of crisis, who would protect us and what sacrifices people would make when 'push came to shove.'

Well, we were shoved. And shoved hard. Those probabilities played themselves out. COVID-19 pulled back the curtain revealing dark corners of our world, our relationships and ourselves. It revealed who the "Little Hitlers" are and the ordinary people who became extraordinary heroes. And it revealed in each of us both our tipping points and the wells of strength that we had, unknowingly, started filling long before.

COVID-19 was a "black swan" event, what I think of as a "Babel moment" that shifted us from our last moment of innocence to something darker but at the same time more raw and more real. It held our feet to the fire, forcing us to confront the messy realities of our world. COVID had a way of hitting particular buttons like no religious or political issue I have known, and the ideological divide it created attained an almost spiritual status. I know couples who weathered the trials of infidelity and bankruptcy and child loss but who separated over COVID-19.

Our world has been turned upside down and we are the unwitting bobble-heads reverberating from every unanticipated new jostle.

MY CHOICE

In 2021, I wrote a book called *My Choice,* a first-hand account of my personal experience with the COVID-19 mandates and my ethical response to them. It was the book I needed to write at the time. It was reactionary and cautionary. We were in the middle of the freedom crisis, and I saw how it was impacting people's lives in immediate and personal ways. I wanted to articulate some of our common instincts so people could approach conversations with loved ones with a fuller arsenal of reasons and reflections, and also to add to the historical record of caution about what these mandates could do to us.

Now, two years later, we have seen how the mandates played out, the effects of the vaccine program on a large scale, the broken relationships, the moral injury. We have seen how our doctors ignored vaccine exemption requests and injury complaints, how our government reacted to the largest public protest in our nation's history. We have seen the scale of government's collusion with Big Tech to suppress medical knowledge that is contrary to state-approved narratives and the echo of this narrative in our highest institutions. And we have seen how differences over these would divide us to the core.

By every single measure, we are a people in crisis. We have an epidemic of homelessness, liquor sales have increased by 55%, anti-anxiety prescriptions are up 34%, and calls to suicide hotlines, suicides themselves, and domestic violence have all dramatically increased since COVID-19 consumed our lives. We are becoming a nation of unhealthy, obese, depressed, sometimes drunken and reliably aimless people. As a young person told me in 2020, "basically no one under 40 thinks that anything good can ever happen again." We have a crisis of trust, a crisis of personal identity, a crisis of community, and a crisis of hope.

I wrote in *My Choice* that, aside from anything else, COVID-19 has created a pandemic of coercion and compliance. Without making any assumptions about its ultimate cause, COVID-19 was a moral litmus test that resulted in the largest compliance test humanity has ever faced, a test we failed on a global scale.

When I wrote *My Choice*, we didn't yet know how many would comply and how many, even now, would feel justified in embracing the government response. We didn't know how many would take their sixth shot after suffering two strokes and contracting COVID…for a third time. We didn't know how many would make risky health choices just to go to bars, play sports, and travel. We didn't know how many would commit to "masking forever," as a well-known social influencer said.

For better or for worse, all of these unknowns have now played out. We have seen the prevalence and the consequences of compliance. We now know who masked without evidence, locked down despite the harms, and vaccinated without asking any of the appropriate "What? How? Why?" questions. We saw just how quickly the majority bypassed any conversations about evidence and necessity, and leaped to do whatever we were told to do, merely because we were told to do it.

Even now, coffee shop talk is noticeably entitled and congratulatory, with an air of the 'What-we-did-worked' mentality that will undoubtedly be invoked in the coming months to expedite an imminent viral response. Those who refused vaccination up to now will be scapegoated to explain why we must go through 'this' all over again.

In my own little corner of the world, masks are slowly reappearing, faded arrows on store floors are catching my eye, school shutdown discussions are resurfacing, and news articles about spikes in infection rates are being released with an alarming regularity.

People are desperate to return to a kind of normal, but with a newfound social caution and an almost forced frivolity, carefully navigating conversations to stick to safe topics like their newest car purchase, our unseasonably wet summer, or the Barbie movie.

COVID-19 was not merely a viral or a discrete event; it was the opportunity to change Canada from a free, energetic, liberal society of neighbours to an authoritarian, collectivist society of broken souls addicted to government edicts and to compliance.

THE 'CAN'T UNSEE' PHENOMENON

Having moved through the intensity of the crisis, we can now step back to reflect on what happened. Why didn't more people demand evidence for the life-altering changes they were about to make? Why were so many so willing — enthusiastic, even — to line up for hours to get shots they knew nothing about? Why weren't more questions asked, especially when it came to masking and distancing our children? Why so much narrative enthusiasm rather than just a rational response to a set of facts? Why were so many more allegiant to their government than to their friends and their own health and well-being? Why did wisdom and independent critical thought have so little power?

Do you know of anyone who spent two or three years fully 'awake,' as they say, and then one day went pro-narrative? Personally, I know no one like this. Why?

I was talking with a friend the other day about an upcoming upholstery project. I have an old chair I would like to recover but I also have a toddler, so I was considering treating the fabric in some way to protect it, but I was also cautious to avoid using harmful chemicals. I mentioned all of this in conversation with my friend who, with reflex speed, responded, well, if it's on the market, it can't be harmful.

If it's on the market, it can't be harmful.

Really? You would think that if any fundamental belief was undermined over the last four years, it would be this. And yet here it stands alive and well, invoked as a standalone premise in an argument. (It's worth mentioning that this is a person with a PhD, two gold medals, and an advanced professional degree.) The air got thick and tense, and we dropped the conversation.

You might be familiar with the psychological phenomenon colloquially called the "can't-unseen phenomenon," also called the "rabbit-duck illusion" meant to illustrate the power of perception. If not, you will surely have seen the image meant to support it.

The "rabbit-duck illusion" refers to an ambiguous image frequently used in psychology to illustrate how perception influences how we process and interpret information from our environment.

The illusion dates back to an 1892 issue of *Fliegende Blatter*, a German humour magazine, later made famous by the philosopher of language Ludwig Wittgenstein in his *Philosophical Investigations*. The idea is that, whichever animal you notice first — the rabbit or the duck — once you become aware that the other animal is also depicted, you can never unsee it.

Another equally powerful example of the illusion is the following image, introduced in the early 1900s by German psychologists. What initially looks like just a series of black and white blotches starts to resolve into a Dalmatian bending down to take a drink. Once the shape emerges, try as you might, you'll never be able to unsee it.

Both illusions are meant to show that we aren't just passive recipients of information from the world around us; rather, we impose a structure on what we see. Our perceptions are informed by our expectations, and frequently by our beliefs about the world.

Neuropsychologists have elaborate explanations for why this happens, appealing to the brain's visual cortex which creates predictions about what the picture might be. Any notion that a duck or rabbit or Dalmatian might be present primes the brain to identify an ambiguous line as the top of an ear or a white stripe as a leg, and so on.[2]

What's interesting is that the images don't change, but once your mind is exposed to new ways of organizing the data, and new ways of imposing that organization on your viewing of it, that will forever influence how you see the image.

With warp speed, COVID-19 propelled us into a world where we were immediately divided into duck-seers and rabbit-seers. And what we saw influenced how we would perceive everything that would transpire over the next three years. If you were primed to believe the narrative, then every piece of new information was seen to hang together with perfect consistency. If you were primed not to believe the narrative, then its irrationality could not be denied.

These two fundamentally different ways of viewing the world are what divide us today:

You either believe that the societal infrastructure we have built has inherent integrity, that our most revered institutions cannot err in their recommendations, and that the decisions we make as a group are better than those we could make on our own, or you don't.

And if you suggest to someone that there might be something more than meets the eye, or even that we are being intentionally deceived or misled, then you are seen as defecting from the collective human project, or you are foolish to question it. And no one wants to be a fool. (But, of course, the great secret of the fool, as Isaac Asimov said, is "that he is no fool at all.")

IS THIS A BOOK ABOUT COVID-19?

Before writing another book, I wanted to come to terms with whether or not I had anything else to say about what transpired over the last four years, whether I had personally learned anything that could help to explain what happened, why it happened, or what we might be able to think or feel or do that could be useful to others.

Of all the things that surprised me over the last four years, the most significant by far is that very little of what happened to us was actually forced on us. Most of us allowed it to happen and many of us even embraced it. No one (as far as I know) was held at gunpoint to be vaccinated. Quebec never did impose the financial penalty for the unvaccinated (though, if they did, it still wouldn't have amounted to outright force). The truth is that most of what happened, happened because people were coerced into it, or because they knowingly and willingly chose it.

For this reason, I have come to be less interested in what was done to us than in how we responded, less interested in data and evidence that undermines the narrative than in why the narrative has been so buoyant despite a lack of reasonable evidence. What interests me most are the broader historical, cultural, and psychological forces that got us to this point. What mistakes did we make? What were *our* moral failings? How did history set us up for 2020? And how did these failings change us and remake us?

This book isn't an attempt to convince the unconvinced. In it, you won't find grand theories of regulatory capture between government and Big Pharma, no mention of conspiracies about Gates, Schwab or the Rockefellers (though I suspect there is a grain of truth to all of them). These are well beyond my areas of expertise, and in a sense they are irrelevant to my interest in why we acted the way we did and what we can do now going forward.

It is more personal than any of this, more microscopic and, in a sense, more macroscopic. I am less interested in governments than in citizens, less in those who try to control us than in the parts of us that, on some level, find comfort in being controlled. I am much more interested in what makes us believe certain things about the world, and in how we act and potentially can recover as moral beings in situations of crisis.

Preparing this book, I struggled a lot with how much it should engage with the particulars of COVID-19. Is what happened to us really about a virus? Yes and no. COVID punctuated a crisis of a certain kind. It's an elephant in the room we can't ignore. But it isn't essential to the tectonic shifts in our culture and morality we experienced. It could just as easily have been a natural disaster, an economic collapse, or a food shortage that punctuated our crisis.

On the other hand, how can one write a book about what's happened over the last four years while sidestepping the issue entirely? It framed every aspect of our lives from employment to law to health to our personal relationships. So my challenge was to navigate the waters between the Scylla and Charybdis of dwelling on the acute but impermanent COVID crisis, on the one hand, and unnaturally avoiding the elephant in the room, on the other.

But in engaging with the COVID crisis, I have chosen to dig deeper, to think not at the level of Big Tech regulatory captures, mid-level policy makers or even global political forces that might have engineered the crisis and our response to it. Many more capable than I have tackled these issues with great acuteness and fluency. My interests are a little more modest, a little closer to home, and yet a little more existential and historically sweeping at the same time.

○ ○ ○

I take it as a given that most of us are immeasurably worse off than we were going into 2020. Our health — physically and mentally — has suffered, our relationships have worn thin, we have lost jobs and homes and educational opportunities and financial stability. The rule of law is feeling shaky, our patriotism is waning and we are, by most testimonies, morally weary.

And if I am right that much of this was brought on by our own compliance, and even by our enthusiasm, the question that stands out for me is why did we do it? Why did we make choices that would turn out to make us worse off than we were, than we needed to be? Why did we bring about our own destruction?

Are we really the victims of a viral crisis or an intentional attempt to make us less free, or are we tragic characters who, despite good intentions, are actually driving our own destruction? Are we living out the tragic stories of Oedipus, Hamlet, and Willy Loman? If so, do we suffer from some tragic character flaw that explains the making of our own destruction?

This book is about our last innocent moment, what we lost, why we lost it and how to recover the lost parts of ourselves. It is a collection of essays which explores the general thesis that COVID-19 was merely a chapter in our tragic story, the natural consequence of a collective tragic character flaw that is slowly destroying us (in our own little lives and as a civilization, more generally). It takes very seriously the idea that we are living out a tragic story in which we are the main characters.

But the story is not all doom and gloom. Like all tragic heroes, we can take control of our circumstances, look our mistakes in the face, and change our trajectory. For literary tragic characters, this involves pain and much effort — what the tragedians called "catharsis," a psychological and moral working out of our flaws — and it's work that our post-WWII coddling hasn't trained us well to do. But embracing our role as tragic characters means that we are less unwitting victims, less puppets in someone else's story, than the heroes of our own. And, as Arthur Miller said, tragedy is inherently optimistic since it is about man's "thrust for freedom."

We are, I believe, standing at a precipice, at a dangerously unprecedented moment in history where we are flirting with the idea of abandoning our right to make decisions about our lives, our bodies, and our children, and with it, we might also be abandoning our civilization and our humanity. Or perhaps we will embrace our rightful place as rational, autonomous beings with the desire and the right and the ability to choose our own lives. This book is for those who understand the difference and choose the second option.

This is a dark time for humanity. But darkness always creates the greatest opportunities for growth and self-awareness, and for us to intentionally remake ourselves for the better. It's time, I believe, that we take back control of our lives, and the responsibility for our choices, and step out onto this precipice without the safety net of an institution or the group on which to download responsibility for our lives. We might misstep, we might free-fall, and we might, dare I say, feel a little uncomfortable and even unsafe at times. But this is, I believe, the only truly human option.

Early on in the process of writing this book, a woman came up to me at a piano recital and said "You made me feel like I wasn't going crazy" (referring to my viral video and public work over the last two years). We all need this. We need to feel like we aren't alone in our suffering, like we share something with the rest of humanity, like we aren't crazy for seeing ducks where others see only rabbits.

SOMEONE LIKE YOU

In every crisis, there's someone like you. Someone who feels that we aren't being told the whole story. Someone who watched the trains creep out of town towards the ghettos thinking something wasn't right. Someone who questions the status quo, who stands up at the dinner party, who raises the uncomfortable question during a phone conversation, who pulls back and carves out time to reflect. Someone who feels a growing unfamiliarity with those around them, who wonders if their intuitions are right or if they really are just crazy.

Whatever you've been through over the last four years, however it has changed you, whatever mistakes you think you might have made, whatever you left unsaid and undone....this book is for you.

My hope is that you will find these essays personally useful and helpful. I hope it will give you the opportunity to work out some things that have been bothering you about what the COVID crisis did to us but also an opportunity to escape from it, to figure out how we can move beyond it and turn our attention to other aspects of our lives that we have neglected. I hope these essays will help you to reflect on the choices you have made, to feel confident in them or to atone for them, and to think about who you want to become.

It will become clear throughout the book that there are two paths you can choose, and there are sacrifices required by both. One is a life of comfort and ease, seeming companionship and apparent safety. The other is a path much less travelled. It comes with deep costs that many have been living out over the last few years. It is a lonely path and one that requires much self-reliance and endurance. But it is the only one that has obvious meaning and purpose, and therefore the only one that will allow you to live in a way that a deep and reflective conscience can tolerate.

It is for those who are looking to put some meat on the bones of your intuitions about what we are going through, who want to be honest about what we have endured and done to each other, and who want to heal it. It is for those who aren't afraid of the messy, grey zones in life, for those who embrace questions without obvious answers. And it is for those who desperately need a space for solace and hope and inspiration in a dark time.

○ ○ ○

The problems that created the COVID crisis are all too human. We have cycled through them before and we will no doubt do so again. They built civilizations and broke them down. Our challenge is, as Walt Whitman said, to "look our times and lands searchingly in the face, like a physician diagnosing some deep disease" so that our tragedies might become a little less acute in future.

And so, here we are at our precipice. The moment is upon us. We can't reclaim the innocence we lost in 2020 but we can use our experiences to remake a more innocent world, for ourselves and for our children. We have a real opportunity to step into our maturity with the lessons of history and with newfound purpose for creating a stable, meaningful, even joyful human life in a rapidly changing world. We can, I dare say, create something even greater.

Ours is a story of self-awakening, a coming of age story. And we are still writing our chapter. We can still change our course. Time will tell if we are failed tragic characters or if we will look our mistakes in the face and embrace who we can be, in all its beautiful imperfections.

I hope you will enjoy taking a journey through these pages, a journey of self-awareness and catharsis and, ultimately, a coming of age. Enlightenment can be around the corner. It can be our legacy. But only if we crave it so desperately that our everyday choices reflect that desire. It is, I promise you, the only way out. And it's the only thing that will save us all.

Yours, in solidarity and in hope,

, PhD

Where Are We Now?

Pretending something doesn't matter doesn't make it matter less.

— Jennifer Lynn Barnes, *All In*

DO YOU MATTER?

"I am Kelly-Sue Oberle. I live at [address]. I belong to someone, and I matter."

These are the words on the slip of paper that Kelly-Sue Oberle places under her pillow every night. The note isn't an affirmation. It isn't a self-help exercise. It is a link to her existence, a literal reminder to her future self of who she is in case she wakes up one day and forgets.

On June 23, 2022, I was at the Citizens' Hearing organized by the Canadian Covid Care Alliance on the 16th floor of a skyscraper in Toronto's financial district, listening to story after story of the harms of the government's COVID-19 response, including many whose lives were impacted by vaccine injury. Kelly-Sue's testimony leaves me shaken even now.

In 2021, Kelly-Sue was an active 68-year-old with a busy work schedule. She walked 10 miles a day and worked 72 hours a week for the charity she founded. She was a typical A-type overachiever and was looking forward to retirement. Sun-bleached and very fit, she was the picture of activity and industriousness. She initially took the Pfizer COVID shot as a manager of 700 volunteers tasked with feeding over 800 children on weekends and holidays to "stay open for them." After her first shot, she experienced pain in her calf and foot and went to a vascular surgeon who informed her that she had blood clots in her femoral artery.

By the time of her diagnosis, Kelly-Sue had already taken the second shot, which left her suffering from a chain of strokes and Transient Ischemic Attacks (TIAs). One stroke left her unsure of who she was after awakening from a nap. She is now blind in one eye.

In her testimony, Kelly-Sue described her doctors as impatient and gruff, one advising her not to return unless she suffered a catastrophic stroke. "Correlation is not causation," she repeatedly heard. In more and less explicit ways, she was told that her experiences don't matter, or at least that they matter less than those who suffered and died from COVID, less than those who fear the virus and follow the narrative.

But Kelly-Sue refuses to be silenced. She refuses to be unseen. She refuses to be a number. Without the validation of others, she has to remind herself every day of who she is. The note she leaves beside her bed is a reminder to herself that she matters.

o o o

At some point over the last two years, you probably wondered if you matter. Maybe you felt like a misfit, a foreigner within a new operating system in which silence is golden, conformity is the social currency, and doing your part is the mark of a good 21st century citizen. Maybe you felt like your government cared less about you than those who chose to follow the narrative. In truth, they probably did.

Without these assurances, you trudged along with the message that you mattered less, that you were devalued and ignored for your choices, that your unwillingness to follow the narrative was leaving you somehow behind. And that is not an insignificant burden to bear. For most, the stigma and bother of questioning this system is too risky, too inconvenient. But for you, it's conformity that is too costly, and the need to question and, possibly resist, too hard to ignore.

I know this operating system well. It is the one that singled me out, expressed its intolerance for my nonconformist ways, and ultimately tried to string me up in the proverbial public square.

In September 2021, I faced what felt like the supreme ethical test: comply with my university's COVID-19 vaccine mandate or refuse and likely lose my job. For better or for worse, I chose the latter. I was quickly and efficiently terminated "with cause." I had spectacularly failed the test according to my colleagues, our public health officials, the *Toronto Star*, the *National Post*, the CBC, and the New York University bioethics professor who said "I wouldn't pass her in my class."

WHAT HAVE WE LEARNED?

When I wrote *My Choice* almost two years ago, my perspective was largely personal and prospective. Few were speaking out, few had been publicly terminated or outed for their COVID-heretical views. Few knew what the price of dissidence would be.

I wrote the book because I was worried. I was worried about what the world would look like if the mandates continued, if the mRNA vaccines were rolled out on a large scale, especially to children and pregnant women. I was worried about the effects on health, certainly, but I was also worried about the new era of medical discrimination we would be ushering into health care and into our collective consciousness, more generally. And I was worried that the mandates would create a division in society that we might never be able to repair.

We no longer have the burden, or the benefit, of relying on worries and educated guesses. We have seen the COVID protocol play out in real time and with real effects on our bodies, our relationships, and our families, and on public trust and civility.

By all measures, the public health response to COVID by every major world government was an unprecedented catastrophe, a tragedy even. We saw the colossal failure of "Zero-COVID," and the effects of waves of masking orders and mandates for employment, education, travel and entertainment. We saw the vaccine program rolled out across all continents, in all age groups, and its effects on individual health and all-cause mortality.

We saw the power of gaslighting, backpedalling, and narrative spin as the science changed. We saw the messaging morph from the directive in 2021 that the 'vaccines' were guaranteed to prevent people from contracting COVID-19 to the more dilute suggestion that the goal all along was merely to minimize the severity of the virus.

We saw our prime minister, Justin Trudeau, impose vaccine mandates for all federal employees in October 2021 and use hatred of the unvaccinated as a successful campaign promise, and then tell a group of students at the University of Ottawa in April 2023 that he was never targeting those who were rationally cautious. We saw our Deputy Prime Minister, Chrystia Freeland, insist on the vaccines' ability to prevent transmission and then a Pfizer Executive admit to the European Parliament in October 2022 that they never tested the vaccine's ability to prevent transmission. (A number of fact-checking articles then emerged to show why it wasn't news that the vaccines didn't perform as advertised.)

We learned that the Trudeau government's vaccine mandates for travel and federal employment were driven by politics and not science, and that the *Emergency Order* was based on narrative hysteria, not evidence of genuine threat. We learned that the federal government has a $105 million contract with the World Economic Forum for the Known Traveler Digital ID, and that China locked down the cities of Wuhan, Huanggang and Echo in January 2020 against the recommendation of the World Health Organization.[3]

On a more personal level, it's been a dizzying year. My daughter, who was born a month after the pandemic was declared, is now three years old. Miraculously, she has learned to walk and talk, to reason and feel and imagine while the world shifted around her.

I've sat for more than 75 interviews, written essays, op-eds, and expert reports for legal cases, and spoken at rallies and events, including the Freedom Convoy in Ottawa. I even returned to Western, the university that terminated me two and a half years ago, to speak on the 'Concrete Beach' at a student-organized rally.

I've spoken with virologists, immunologists, cardiologists, nurses, lawyers, politicians, historians, psychologists, philosophers, journalists, musicians, and athletes. My YouTube content generated over a million views and 18 million Twitter impressions.

But more importantly than any of that, I met you. I looked in your eyes, I shook your hands, I saw the trauma of loss and abandonment on your faces, and I heard your stories.

We leaned in for a hug over the broccoli tower at the grocery store when tears started to well up in our eyes. We exchanged knowing looks when we met at rallies and events, at the dog park, and once even at the gas pump. That look of 'You get it,' 'I see you,' of someone who sees that something fundamental has shifted in the world and we may never be able to go back.

I learned how easy it is for us to betray one another and how COVID exposed the fault lines in our relationships. But I also saw humanity all around. I saw hugs and connection and immense warmth everywhere I went. I saw the worst side of humanity and the best, and I witnessed the indomitable power of inconvenient truths. The COVID-19 battleground has certainly created its heroes and villains, and we have all taken sides about which is which.

I had the honour to interview and be interviewed by some of the best, those the world has vilified. Below is just a snapshot of the insights they offered that struck me the moment I heard them:

- Zuby: "This is the first pandemic in history where a significant number of people want it to be worse than it is."

- Jordan Peterson: "The truth isn't a set of facts. The truth is an approach to dialogue and discussion."

- Bruce Pardy: "The law is the product of the culture and, as the culture moves, so does the law. In our case, the legal culture has been changing for decades."

- Bret Weinstein: "We had something deeply flawed but highly functional. Something that could have been repaired. And instead of looking at what was wrong with it, and being realistic about how to fix it, and at what rate we could reasonably expect it to get better, we foolishly allowed ourselves to become unmoored. And I don't think people have yet understood how dangerous it is to be unmoored in history. We have cut ourselves loose and we are now adrift. And what we cannot say is where we will land."

- Michael Driver: "There's a lovely line from Canadian poet Mark Strand, which is that 'If we knew how long the ruins would last we would never complain.' This is it. This is the moment that we have as humans. There is no alternative to optimism. The ruins of our lives won't last for an eternity after we're gone. This is it."

- Trish Wood: "The people who were awake first took the biggest risks. In my view, they were all people who are deeply, deeply humane."

- Susan Dunham: "Since 9/11, every threat to come down the mainstream news cycle seemed to huddle us around the same consensus, that some fresh element of our liberty was making the world hurt and that we were selfish to hold on to it."

Mattias Desmet: "The people who are not in the grip of mass formation, who typically try to wake the people up who are in the mass formation, usually won't succeed. But… if these people continue to speak out, their dissonant voice will constantly disturb the hypnotizing voice of the leaders of the masses and they will make sure that the mass formation doesn't go so deep…. Historical examples show that it is exactly at the moment that the dissonant voices stop speaking out in public spaces that the destruction campaigns started that happened in 1930 in the Soviet Union, in 1935 in Nazi Germany."

You may have noticed that few of these comments are directly related to COVID-19 science or politics. They are about human nature, our weaknesses and inclinations, history, culture, and how these brought us to this particular place and time.

You've probably learned a lot about yourself over the last two years, what you are able to tolerate and endure, what sacrifices you are willing to make, and where you draw your line in the sand. As I write this, I wonder about your stories: What are your experiences of alienation and cancellation? How has your thinking evolved over the last four years? What have you lost that is irrecoverable? What relationships have you found that wouldn't have been possible without it? What allows you to weather the storms of shame and ostracization when others can't? What keeps you on the road less travelled?

Over the last year, my perspective has changed a lot, morphing from future to present and past tense, and I wonder, Where are we now? How did we get here?

What I think about these days has little to do with data or science. We have all drawn our battle lines on those fronts and we aren't seeing much movement across them. The pro-narrative position is alive and well. Conversions are uncommon and mass revelations unlikely. Furthermore, I don't think the situation in which we find ourselves was generated by a miscalculation of the data but by a crisis of the values and ideas that led to it.

○ ○ ○

Since writing the book, I've had a lot of time to think about whether my original reasoning was sound, whether my prospective concerns bore out. Given the numbers against me, I must admit that my confidence ebbs and flows. With the exception of maybe two or three other ethicists *in the world*, I alone challenged the mandates. Was I wrong? Did I overlook something obvious?

I try very hard to be alive to this possibility. But every time I run the argument in my head, I return to the same place. And in this place, two years later, it is now even more clear to me that the COVID response was a global failure from which we will be recovering for decades, and maybe centuries.

What we learned over the last year only confirms, and intensifies, my initial thinking. We learned that the vaccines are doing exactly what the clinical trials indicated they would do, which is fail to prevent transmission and increase mortality in the vaccine group. As a paper by some of the world's top scientists and bioethicists shows, 22,000-30,000 healthy adults aged 18-29 would need to be boosted with an mRNA vaccine to prevent one COVID-19 hospitalization and, to prevent that one hospitalization, there would be 18-98 serious adverse events.[4] (Incidentally, this is the age of most students at Western, the last university in the country to lift their COVID vaccine mandate.) We learned that countries with the highest vaccination rates have the highest COVID and death rates. And, as of August 2023, the CDC is reporting excess mortality for ages 0-24 at 44.8% above historical levels, a super-disaster given that a 10 percent rise is a once in 200-year disastrous event.[5]

WINNING AT THE WRONG GAME IS STILL LOSING

The evidence undeniably shows that the government response to COVID-19, the mandates in particular and especially for young people, are unjustified on a cost-benefit analysis. But I worry that trying to show they are unjustified is playing the wrong game, and winning at the wrong game is still losing. Acquiescence to medical coercion would be unethical *even if* the vaccine was a harmless placebo. To see this, think for a minute about what a mandate does which is, essentially, to divide people into three groups:

1. Those who would have done what the mandate demands even without it, making the mandate unnecessary.
2. Those who wouldn't do what the mandate demands even with it, making the mandate ineffective.
3. Those who choose to do what the mandate demands only because of it, which makes their choice coerced, something we have spent seventy-five years since Nuremberg trying to understand and avoid.

The crucial element of informed consent that has been overlooked for the last four years is that it is not about what's best from an objective point of view.

Consent is personal. It is about some particular person's deeply held beliefs and values, and it should reflect the risks *that particular person* is willing to take. A judge made this point in a case (a case which was eventually overturned by the Supreme Court) involving a twelve-year-old trying to resist her father's request to be vaccinated when he wrote: "Even if I were to take judicial notice of the 'safety' and 'efficacy' of the vaccine, I still have no basis for assessing what that means for *this* child."

Furthermore, most arguments in favour of informed consent and autonomy over compliance, and most responses to these arguments, focus on the moral significance of risk of harm. Arguments claiming that we have a moral obligation to vaccinate, for example, claim that we have an obligation to reduce the risk to the health of others by accepting an increased or unknown health risk to ourselves. And even arguments against the mandates tend to proceed on the basis that novel vaccine technologies impose an undue burden of risk of harm to the patient.

But, as ethicist Michael Kowalik points out, because mandatory vaccination violates bodily autonomy, it constitutes not merely a risk of harm but an *actual* harm to any person made to accept vaccination under duress. When we aren't able to make our own choices, or to act on the choices we have made, we are harmed. This doesn't mean we can always do just whatever we want to do. Some choices are practically impossible to execute (e.g. we want to fly off a high cliff unassisted) while others are too costly to others (e.g. we want to go on a wanton stealing spree), but the crucial point to realize is that overriding individual choice is harmful, even in cases where it might be shown to be justified.

So the ethics of forced or coerced vaccination isn't a matter of balancing risk of harm to self versus risk of negative health effects to others; these are distinct moral categories. Forcing a person to be vaccinated against her will, or even undermining the consent process that would make a fully informed choice possible affects, as Kowalik says, "the ontological dimensions of personhood."

In spite of all of this, the "Do your part" narrative is alive and well and, with it, the obfuscation of consent, the central pillar of medical care.

IN PLAIN SIGHT

There is no doubt that the government response to COVID-19 is the largest public health disaster in modern history.

But what most interests and worries me is not that the authorities demanded our compliance, not that the media failed to ask the right questions, but that we submitted so freely, that we were so easily seduced by the assurance of safety over freedom, and the invitation to applaud shame and hatred of the non-compliant.

What shocks me still is that so few fought back.

And so the question that keeps me up at night is, how did we get to this place? Why didn't we know?

I think part of the answer, the part that is hard to process, is that we did know. Or at least the information that would have allowed us to know was hiding in plain sight.

In 2009, Pfizer (the company we are told exists to "change patients' lives" and "make the world a healthier place"[6]) received a record-setting $2.3 billion fine for illegally marketing its painkiller Bextra and for paying kickbacks to compliant doctors. At the time, associate U.S. attorney general Tom Perrelli said the case was a victory for the public over "those who seek to earn a profit through fraud."

Well, yesterday's victory is today's conspiracy theory. And, unfortunately, Pfizer's misstep is not a moral anomaly in the pharmaceutical industry.

Those familiar with the history of psychopharmacology will know of the drug industry's profile of collusion and regulatory capture: the Thalidomide disaster of the 1950s and 1960s, the Opioid epidemic of the 1980s, Anthony Fauci's mismanagement of the AIDS epidemic, the SSRI crisis of the 1990s, and that just scratches the surface. The fact that drug companies are not moral saints should never have surprised us.

So why didn't that knowledge get the traction it deserved? How did we get to the point where our blind adherence to "follow the science" ideology led us to be more unscientific than arguably at any other moment in history?

HOW MUCH FREEDOM IS YOUR SAFETY WORTH?

If you heard one of my speeches over the last couple of years, you might be familiar with the parable of the camel.

On a cold night in the desert, a man is sleeping in his tent, having tied his camel outside. As the night grows colder, the camel asks his master if he can put his head in the tent for warmth. "By all means," says the man; and the camel stretches his head into the tent. A little while later, the camel asks if he may also bring his neck and front legs inside. Again, the master agrees.

Finally, the camel, who is now half in, half out, says "I'm letting cold air in. May I not come inside?" With pity, the master welcomes him into the warm tent. But once inside, the camel says. "I think that there is not room for both of us here. It will be best for you to stand outside, as you are the smaller." And with that the man is forced outside of his tent.

Let me put my head in, then my neck and front legs, then my whole self. Then, please step outside. Wear the arm-band, show your papers, pack a suitcase, move to the ghetto, pack another suitcase, get on the train. "Arbeit Macht Frei" until you find yourself in a lineup for the gas chamber.

How does this happen?

The camel's lesson is that you can get people to do just about anything if you break the unreasonable down into a series of smaller, seemingly reasonable 'asks.' It is the humble petition of the camel—just to put his head in the tent—that is so modest, so pitiful, that it seems unreasonable to refuse.

Isn't this what we've seen over the last two years?

It's been a master class in how to influence a person's behaviour one step at a time by encroaching a tiny bit, pausing, then starting from this new place and encroaching again, all the while unwittingly transferring what matters to us most to whoever is coercing us.

This idea that our liberties are something authorities can wantonly suspend is reflected in the eery reasoning of British epidemiologist Neil Ferguson, who said this about what inspired his recommendation of the lockdowns:

"I think people's sense of what is possible in terms of control changed quite dramatically between January and March... We couldn't get away with it in Europe, we thought.... And then Italy did it. And we realized we could."[7]

We got to this point because we consented to tiny encroachments that we never should have consented to, not because of the size but the nature of the ask. When we were first asked to lock down but had questions, we should have refused. When doctors were first asked to deny available therapeutics for COVID, they should have refused. Today's physicians who are ordered to follow the CPSO's guideline to prescribe psycho-pharmaceuticals and psychotherapy for vaccine-hesitant patients should object.

We got to this point not because we consider autonomy to be a reasonable sacrifice for the public good (although there are surely some of us who do). We got to this point because we are suffering from "moral blindness," a term ethicists apply to those who would otherwise act ethically but because of temporary pressures (like a coercive medical body or a myopic obsession to "do our part"), and are therefore temporarily unable to see the harms we do.

How can little things like autonomy and consent possibly stack up against saving the human race? How could freedom possibly win out over purity, safety, and perfection?

o o o

In *My Choice*, I wrote about the nudge paradigm (based on the 2008 book, *Nudge*), a form of behavioural psychology that uses the active engineering of choice to influence our behaviour in barely discernible ways. I have since learned much more about how most major governments employed this paradigm in their COVID response.

Behavioural insights teams like MINDSPACE (UK) and Impact Canada are tasked not only with tracking public behaviour and sentiment, but planning ways to shape it in accordance with public health policies. These "nudge units" are composed of neuroscientists, behavioural scientists, geneticists, economists, policy analysts, marketers, and graphic designers. Members of Impact Canada include Dr. Lauryn Conway, who focuses on "the application of behavioural science and experimentation to domestic and international policy;" Jessica Leifer, who is a self-control and willpower specialist; and Chris Soueidan, a graphic designer responsible for developing the Impact Canada's digital brand.

Slogans like "Do your part," hashtags such as #COVIDVaccine and #postcovidcondition, images of nurses donning masks that look like something from the movie *Outbreak*, and even the soothing jade green colour on the "Get the facts about COVID-19 vaccines" fact-sheets are all products of Impact Canada's research and marketing gurus.

Even the steady flow of more subtle images in familiar places (on electronic traffic signs and in YouTube ads) of masks, syringes, and vaccine bandaids, normalizes the behaviour through the subtle suggestion and justification of fear and purity consciousness.

With greater than 90 percent reported vaccination rates in some countries, the efforts of the world's nudge units seem to have been wildly successful. But why were we so susceptible to being nudged in the first place? Aren't we supposed to be the rational, critical-thinking descendants of the Enlightenment? Aren't we supposed to be scientific?

Of course, the majority of those who were following the narrative thought they were being scientific. They thought they were "following the science" by reading *The Atlantic* and the *New York Times*, and listening to CBC and CNN. The fact that media articles might have contained obfuscated, missing, and misleading data, as well as intimidating, often shaming, language from those deemed medical "experts," never appeared as conflicted with their view that they were being scientific.

THE FEAR FACTOR

One of the great lessons of the last four years is just how powerfully we are all affected by fear, how it can alter our capacities for critical thinking and emotional regulation, shifting us to abandon existing beliefs and commitments, and become irrationally pessimistic.

We saw how fear makes us particularly susceptible to the media's negative framing that focuses on case and death numbers and not on the fact that, for most, COVID causes only mild symptoms. We saw how fear reframes how we relate to one another, making us more suspicious, more ethnocentric, more intolerant, more hostile toward out-groups, and more susceptible to a saviour stepping in (think of Canada's Transport Minister frequently claiming that everything the government has done over last two years is to "keep you safe").

We are also starting to understand how our manipulated fears caused the mass hysteria to set in, and how our moral panic was generated in the first place. Parents are still paranoid that their children are at great risk from COVID even though in Canada not one child has died from COVID without a comorbidity.

Our fear didn't develop naturally. The nudging didn't emerge *ex nihilo* in 2020. Our blindness, our reflex to persecute those who threatened our ideas of purity, is the culmination of a long-term cultural revolution and devolution of all the institutions we trust so deeply: government, law, media, medical colleges and professional bodies, academia, and private sector industries. It would take a book to explore all the ways our institutions have undergone a synchronized implosion over the last several decades. Maybe I'll write that book one day.

But for now, I think of how prescient were the words of Antonio Gramsci who said that to achieve a wholesale shift in thinking, we must "capture the culture." Couple this with Rudi Dutschke's exhortation to take a "long march through the institutions" and you have the perfect recipe for the cultural revolution that brought us to this point.

Each of the core institutions that we have been trained to trust was transformed by a paradigm shift in values, a shift towards the "politics of intent" which assumes that, if your intentions are noble and your compassion boundless, you are virtuous, even if your actions ultimately lead to disaster on a colossal scale. Those who refuse to surrender moral turf to the so-called 'progressives' are shamed or cancelled into oblivion so that the Utopian world of absolute purity can be realized.

This is the social operating system that has proven its ability to reshape society without limitation, that led to my termination, that tells Kelly-Sue Oberle "correlation isn't causation," that upheld the suspension of Dr. Crystal Luchkiw for giving a COVID vaccine exemption to a high-risk patient, that led you to read the words on this page now. And the fallout from this progressive shift is the moral blindness that plagues us now, the hijacked moral consciences, the belief that our compliance is harmless or even impeccably virtuous.

SOME INTERNAL JUGGLING

Now in my forties, my birth date is unfathomably closer to the end of WWII than to today's date. I feel young, all things considered. I certainly haven't lived long enough for humanity to forget the lessons of our greatest human atrocity.

I was born the month Saigon fell, signalling the end of the Vietnam War. I have lived through the Columbine massacre, 9/11 and the invasion of Iraq, the Rwandan and Darfur genocides, the War in Afghanistan, and the rape and murderous spree of Ted Bundy, but I experienced nothing that presented a crisis on so many fronts, creating so much personal and global instability, as what transpired over the last four years.

I mentioned in the introduction that people like myself, who question the narrative, are considered foolish for doing so. Foolish not just because we are presumed wrong but because we are assumed dangerous, that our failure to see things the "right way" poses a risk to others.

I have often wondered if I am a fool. I am many things: a former philosophy professor, a reluctant public intellectual, a wife, a mother, a friend. But I am also the noise in the study, the outlier, the nonconformist, the kink in the collectivist agenda. I am the one who cares more about being able to sleep at night than fitting in.

What makes me different? I really don't know.

I can say that I have experienced more internal juggling over the last four years than at any other point in my life. The stakes were high. They are high. And, alongside my very public work, I underwent much personal transformation. I became a mother, which has been the most personally transformative experience of my life.

To see and feel these two parallel experiences — the personal and the public — weave in and out of one another has been both exhausting and as authentic as any could be. The experience leaves me feeling mentally emaciated and invigorated at the same time, while the waves of new challenges roll over me on a daily basis. And I wonder every day if I have been made better or worse by them, or if I am just different than I would have been without them.

When I first stepped onto this battlefield three years ago, I felt fiery and equipped with as much energy as I would ever need to fight this fight. But, in late fall 2022, it all stopped. The well of energy dried up. I hosted an event for The Democracy Fund with Conrad Black interviewing Jordan Peterson in Toronto and, while waiting to go on stage, I had the feeling it would be my last public event. I had drained the resources that made public appearances possible. I was fighting a war I didn't understand. The energy output felt futile. I couldn't imagine that yet another Zoom call would make a difference. Offers from ever-more popular freedom personalities came rolling in but it all felt insignificant, and I felt foolish for thinking that any of it mattered. In early 2023, I felt battle-weary and mentally drained. To be uncomfortably honest, I wanted to retreat, to recoil to my own little corner of the world, and shut out the eerie chaos around me.

Even now, I struggle with how to balance my obligations to my family with having a more public role. I wonder what I've lost and what life would have been like without the crisis. And,

I resent the time this fight takes away from being able to enjoy my daughter's childhood and to relive my own through hers. It's hard to leave this peaceful, playful world and step yet another day onto the battlefield.

People often ask what moves me. In *My Choice*, I talked about being a hardcore individualist who sees consensus as a 'red flag' about what to avoid. But there is something even more basic than this. I love truth and I love my daughter. And I want to create a world for her in which she never needs to make the sacrifices I'm making now. In which she can make daisy chains without worrying about the next lockdown, and read to her children without thinking about digital passports.

It's not a coincidence, I think, that so many of the freedom fighters are parents, the ones who are most motivated for the fight but have the least time and energy for it. We are the ones who see the future in our children's eyes, who have a vision of what their lives will be like if we do nothing. And we can't bear to have this world be our children's future.

WHERE TO FROM HERE?

So how do we cure this moral blindness? How do we wake up to the harms of what we are doing?

Though it pains me to say, I don't think reason is going to do it. The last few years have proven philosopher David Hume right, that "reason is and ought only to be a slave of the passions." I have yet to hear of someone being convinced of the absurdity of the COVID narrative on the basis of reason or evidence alone. I worked for months with the Canadian Covid Care Alliance to provide evidence-based information about COVID-19 but I didn't see any real effect until I made a video in which I cried.

In saying that, I don't mean to disparage the importance of rigorous scientific evidence or to elevate careless rhetoric. But what I have learned from speaking with thousands of you at events and protests, in interviews and over email is that my video had resonance not because of any particular thing I said but because you felt my emotion: "I cried with you," you said. "You showed what we were all feeling." "You spoke to my heart." And that's what made the difference.

Why did you cry when you saw that video? Why do tears well up over broccoli at the grocery store? Because, I think, none of this is about data and evidence and reason; it's about feelings, good or bad. Feelings that justify our purity culture, feelings that motivate our virtue signals, feelings that we have been told we don't matter, feelings that, for all our efforts, there will one day be no sign that we ever walked on this earth.

You were responding not to my reasons but to my humanity. You saw in me another person embracing what you felt, reaching out across the gulf to connect with the meaning we all share. The lesson we can learn is a confirmation of the Belgian psychologist Mattias Desmet's exhortation to keep reaching for what we all deeply crave: meaning, common ground, connecting with the humanity in others. And that's how we have to continue to fight.

Do facts matter? Of course they do. But facts, alone, will never be able to answer the questions we really need to ask. The real ammunition of the COVID war is not information. It's not a battle over what is true, what counts as misinformation, what it means to #followthescience. It's a battle over what our lives mean and, ultimately, whether we matter.

Kelly-Sue needs to tell herself that she matters at a time when the world won't listen. She needs to testify to her own story until it registers on our cultural radar. She needs to speak for those who can't speak for themselves.

In telling herself she matters, she has already done all any of us can do. She has found meaning and purpose; now she just needs to get on with the life of pursuing it, as we all must do.

What Killed
Informed Consent?

Every human being of adult years and sound mind has a right to determine what shall be done with his own body.

—Justice Benjamin Cardozo, *Schloendorff v. Society of New York Hospital (1914)*

IN THE BLINK OF AN EYE

As my fingers type these words in a corner of my local coffee shop, some simple interactions catch my attention.

Could I have a tall dark roast, please? Certainly.
Would you like your croissant warmed up? No, thank you.
Is the milk organic? Of course.

In a few simple exchanges over a morning coffee order, each customer managed to make more robustly informed choices than most did over the far more impactful health and policy issues of the last four years.

Why, I wonder, couldn't we muster the relatively meagre skills of paying attention, asking questions, and expressing a reflective "yes" or "no" when it came to the life-impacting issues of the pandemic — masking, lockdowns, family distancing, and vaccination — when we seem to do it as a matter of course in the more prosaic areas of our lives?

During the pandemic, informed consent was inverted for all to see. The public health establishment concluded that protecting the "greater good" required exceptional measures, making informed consent expendable in the name of "keeping people safe."

Physicians refused to sign exemptions and courts refused to hear exemption requests. Patients were fired for questioning vaccination. Families and social groups began to distill their membership in more and less overt ways, shaming and uninviting until those who remained were pressured into compliance or exile.

And various institutions began to release statements amending their position on informed consent, claiming that its revision was necessitated by the pressures of the pandemic. The FDA and the Office for Human Research Protections, for example, released statements revising their informed consent policies in the wake of the Public Health Emergency Declaration (issued in January 31, 2020, then renewed through May 11, 2023.)

In more and less formal ways, COVID was the tool that transformed our supposedly inalienable right to make informed choices about our private lives into a public and readily dispensable good. It was almost as if we had built such a network of infinitesimal choices creating the powerful illusion of choice that we didn't notice when we were asked to give it all up in an instant. After all, if we can choose to have our coffee prepared and personalized to our liking — if the world is responsive to our needs and desires to *that* degree — why would it occur to us that we can't make decisions about what goes into our bodies?

When I look back over the motley collection of oversights and transgressions of the last four years, what surprises me most is that we let it all happen. The government could have demanded our unquestioning compliance, journalists could have spun a one-sided narrative, and citizens could have shamed us, but we could have resisted it all by simply making our own choices in our own little corners of the world. This should have been the fail-safe that would have put us in a very different place now.

Instead, COVID became a moral litmus test in which we not only showed our capacity for making poor choices but, even more devastatingly, our capacity for complete deference (what some call "public trust"). COVID created an atmosphere in which informed consent simply could not survive. "Free choice" was considered "free riding," and those who made individual choices that departed from what was perceived to "keep people safe" were seen as benefiting from others' sacrifices without incurring costs themselves. As Canadian singer-songwriter Jann Arden quipped in a 2023 podcast, "[V]accinated people have enabled everybody on this planet to be having the lives right now that they're having."

What I would like to do here is to explore what has happened since 2020 that made us so willing to give up personal choice and informed consent so we can better understand how we got to this place and how to prevent the next moral misstep. The answer may surprise you.

WHY DID WE GIVE IN SO EASILY?

Though it might feel like we abandoned our right to make choices in the blink of an eye, informed consent started to lose its footing in medicine, and in culture more generally, in the years leading up to 2020.

Almost 20 years before COVID, ethicist Onora O'Neill callously wrote that "informed consent procedures in medicine […] are useless for selecting public health policies."[8] Her idea was that public health policies must be uniform to be effective, and allowing for personal choice creates the possibility of divergence. For O'Neill, there can be no exceptions regarding individuals' masking or vaccination choices, for example, *and* success at limiting the spread of a lethal virus. You can either have safety *or* individual choice and, when the two conflict, informed consent must give way to the more important value of safety.

When I was a graduate student studying medical ethics in the early 2000s, the value of informed consent was so obvious that it was treated almost as a *prima facie* good, as something with great moral weight. Its value was grounded in the fundamental belief – a belief with deep philosophical roots – that all humans are rational, autonomous (or self-governing) persons who deserve respect. And one of the basic ways of respecting a person is to respect the choices persons make.

As the President's Commission for the Study of Ethical Problems in Medicine and Biomedical and Behaviour Research stated: "Informed consent is rooted in the fundamental recognition — reflected in the legal presumption of competency—that adults are entitled to accept or reject health care interventions on the basis of their own personal values and in furtherance of their own personal goals."[9]

In medical ethics, informed consent became the principal mechanism to prevent some of the most deplorable abuses of human rights: the Tuskegee Syphilis Experiment, the Skid Row Cancer Study, the Stanford Prison Experiment, the GlaxoSmith-Kline and U.S. Military hepatitis E vaccine study, and of course the Nazi Party's medical experimentation and sterilization programs.

With these cautions and philosophical views of personhood in mind, informed consent became the cornerstone of medical ethics with the requirements that the patient (i) must be competent to understand and decide, (ii) receives full disclosure, (iii) comprehends the disclosure, (iv) acts voluntarily, and (v) consents to the proposed action.[10]

These conditions became more or less repeated in every major bioethics document: the Nuremberg Code,[11] The Declarations of Geneva and Helsinki, the 1979 Belmont Report, the Universal Declaration on Bioethics and Human Rights.[12] The Canadian Medical Protective Association document on informed consent says, for example, "For consent to serve as a defence to allegations of either negligence or assault and battery,…[t]he consent must have been voluntary, the patient must have had the capacity to consent and the patient must have been properly informed."

By this standard, how many physicians in Canada were guilty of "negligence or assault and battery" by pushing COVID vaccination on their patients? For how many was the act of COVID vaccination truly voluntary? How many Canadians received full disclosure about the benefits and harms of wearing masks and locking down?

More generally, what if we had just asked more questions? What if we paused to think? What if we listened more than we talked? What if we worked our own way through the evidence instead of simply trusting the 'experts?' As it was, we masked enthusiastically, we locked down hard, and we lined up for hours to get our chance at a shot we knew little about. And amidst it all, there was an eerie absence of questioning and choice.

○ ○ ○

To understand how we got to where we are, it is helpful first to appreciate that informed consent is a relatively recent trend in the history of medicine. Two ancient ideas, which are now exerting a renewed pull on our healthcare system, helped to resist it for a long time.

The first is the idea that the physician or "expert" always knows best (what is referred to in healthcare as "medical paternalism"). The second is the related idea that the value of "the greater good" sometimes supersedes that of patient choice. Both allow that there are things of moral value that can, in principle, override patient choice.

Dating back to Ancient Greece, the dominant trend in patient care was paternalism, which left little room for informed consent and even justified deception. For thousands of years, medical decision-making was almost exclusively the physician's domain whose responsibility it was to inspire confidence in his or her patients. It was the physician who decided whether to withhold a course of antibiotics, to consider a newborn with birth defects a stillbirth, or to give one patient rather than another access to surgery when resources were scarce. Even during the Enlightenment, when new theories of personhood framed patients as rational beings with the capacity to understand their medical options and make their own choices, deception was still felt to be necessary to facilitate patient care.

It wasn't until the 1850s that English Common Law started to reflect worries about injuries incurred from surgery without proper consent. The courts increasingly interpreted a physician's failure to provide adequate information to the patient about his or her treatment as a breach of duty. This trend culminated in the 1914 case of *Schloendorff v. Society of New York Hospital*, which was the first to establish that the patient is an active participant in the treatment decision process. The judge in the case, Justice Benjamin Cardozo, stated:

> *every human being of adult years in sound mind has a right to determine what shall be done with his own body; and a surgeon who performs an operation without his patients consent commits a battery for which he is liable in damages.*[13]

In spite of all of this progress on the autonomy front, informed consent lost its footing in recent years due to an increasingly impersonal health care system congested by a growing number of stakeholders (including public health agencies and the pharmaceutical industry), overworked clinicians, financial conflicts of interest, and shifts in moral and political ideologies. Gradually, almost imperceptibly, the traditional relationships of trust between particular physicians and patients wore thin, and the expectation of explicit consent gave way first to more tacit understandings of the concept and then to its near total erosion.

How could this happen? Why did we experience such a wholesale amnesia for the ethical framework that we had worked so hard to build? What could have made us abandon it all so quickly and so completely?

SCIENTISM IN THE AGE OF COVID

It is said that ours is an age of entitlement, or at least that millennials — the "Me, me, me," generation — have an attitude of entitlement.[14] Our culture caters and markets so fully to every whim that a desire for making our own choices is the last thing you might expect us to give up on. So why did we give up on it?

I believe that the decline of informed consent has coincided not just with the specific events related to COVID-19, but more generally with the ascent of a particular scientific ideology called "scientism."

It's important to be clear that scientism is not science. In fact, it has very little to do with science, itself. It is an ideology, a way of viewing the world that reduces all complexities, and all knowledge, to a single explanatory approach. At its most benign, scientism offers a complete view of the human condition, appealing to science to explain who we are, why we do what we do, and why life is meaningful. It is a meta-scientific view about what science is capable of and how it should be viewed relative to other areas of inquiry including history, philosophy, religion, and literature. Scientism has become so ubiquitous that it now influences every sphere of life from politics to economic policy to spirituality. And, like every dominating ideology that has imposed itself on the world, scientism has its own shamans and wizards.

The practical upshot of this is that, because scientism uses science to resolve conflicts outside its proper domain, conversations about whether it is right to disinvite an unvaccinated sibling from Thanksgiving dinner, for example, frequently devolve into the rhetorical "What, don't you believe in science?" The question assumes that science, by itself, can answer all relevant questions, including those about etiquette, civility, and morality. Hurt feelings, broken relationships, and moral missteps are all justified by appealing to the fact that the shunned individual excused herself from moral consideration by not following "the science."

One particularly devastating feature of scientism is that it obliterates debate and discussion, ironically hallmarks of the scientific method. Think of the frequent invocation of "#Trustthescience" or even just "#Science" in social media communications, used not as a prelude to argument and the presentation of scientific evidence but as a stand-in for them, rendering alternative viewpoints impotent and heretical.

Political scientist Jason Blakely identifies the locus of this feature of scientism as the "overextension of scientific authority." As Blakely wrote in his cover story for Harper's Magazine in August 2023, "scientific expertise has encroached on domains in which its methods are unsuited to addressing, let alone resolving, the issue at hand." The fact that a microbiologist understands the elements of DNA is, today, unquestionably used to grant that person supreme authority in matters of morality and public policy.

The emergence in 2020 of a viral crisis, the proper domain of science, meant the overextension of scientific principles into the sociopolitical and moral domains, and therefore the suspension of all basic ways of treating one another. The assertion made by officials that the pandemic necessitated a specific policy response was a way of suppressing the more complicated ethical and political disagreements that underlaid them. Having suspended our civility, Yale sociologist and physician Nicholas Christakis remarked, "We allowed thousands of people to die alone," and we baptized and buried people by Zoom while the compliant dined out and went to Maroon 5 concerts.[15]

As this transition unfolded, scientism's fundamentalist nature was gradually being exposed. Having emerged as an intolerance to what some perceived as dogmatic, often faith-based ways of viewing the world, scientism called for a return to science to unseat these purportedly "outmoded" systems of belief. But, in so doing, scientism demanded perfect adherence to its own orthodoxy, which ironically led to the resurgence of paternalism that defined the dark ages of medicine.

A sign of this is the near perfect global homogeneity of the COVID response. If individual jurisdictions were allowed to debate and develop their own COVID strategies, we would have undoubtedly seen more varied pandemic responses based on their unique histories, population profiles and what sociologists call "local knowledge." Communities with young families and university students, where the risk of COVID was low but the risk to mental health from lockdowns, closures, and distancing was high, might have opted for more minimal COVID policies. A religious community might have accommodated more risks to attend worship services while commuter-belt communities could have more easily embraced work-from-home restrictions with little negative impact. Every Canadian community would have been allowed to wrestle with the scientific realities of a viral threat balanced against their own values, priorities, and demographics. And the result, varied as it surely would have been, would have created control groups that would have shown the relative successes of different strategies. As it was, we had little opportunity to understand what things would have been like if we had acted differently, and therefore little opportunity to improve our strategies for the future. And, where those opportunities did exist (e.g. in Sweden and Africa), their responses didn't register because they were simply assumed to be unsuccessful as a matter of principle because they departed from the narrative.

As it was, the pandemic response ignored and silenced dissenters in all sectors of society: whistleblowing professionals, concerned parents, and hesitant citizens. We were simply informed of the 'scientifically' appropriate policy, and then nudged and pressured until we complied with it. There was no attempt to engage with the population within the parameters of the pandemic restrictions; no outdoor town hall meetings, no phone polls or online referenda to increase engagement between public servants and those they were supposed to represent. I don't think it would be an exaggeration to say that population lockdown without presentation of evidence, and without discussion and debate, meant not only the dissolution of representative government but the loss any semblance of a robust democracy.

One thing that is crucial to understand about the effects of scientism on the COVID narrative is that those holding 'correct,' pro-narrative views were not as protected by those views as it seemed. Those who followed 'the narrative' enjoyed only the facade of respect because their views weren't conspicuous in the landscape of conformity. The opinions of your friends who masked, distanced, and got boosted to the precise tempo of public health orders were only coincidentally acceptable. If the narrative had changed, those views would have become — and *will* become, if the narrative changes — immediately unacceptable, and their holders shamed and rejected.

In all this we got so much so very wrong. As the philosopher Hans-Georg Gadamer observed, the chief task of a humanistic approach to politics is, first, to guard against "the idolatry of scientific method." Science should inform public health policy, to be sure. But there are important differences between facts and values, the humility with which a scientist tests a hypothesis and the certainty with which a politician asserts a claim. And we must be careful not to conflate our obligations as citizens with our obligations as spouses, parents, siblings, and friends.

Furthermore, science offers no special insight into matters of ethical and political significance. There is no branch of science — no immunology or microbiology — that can determine what makes life meaningful, no way for scientists to prioritize the moral values we ought to have just as there is no scientific 'key' capable of unlocking answers to questions about what it means to be good and live well.

YOUR CHOICE

"Your." "Choice."

Who could have guessed prior to 2020 just how controversial these two little words would become. Simple on their own but, put together, they create an affirmation of yourself, your worth and your abilities, and a declaration of your right to be the author of your own life. They give you the confidence to reflect, consider, question, and resist, and in so doing, make yourself and your place in the world.

To choose is not just to randomly opt for one option over another. It is not an act of indulgence nor is it selfish. It defines who and what we are, as individuals and as a people. In one act of choice, we bring to fruition a lifetime of self-development. In one act of choice, we become human.

As it is, our scientism has put us into a moral deficit that is destroying our own moral capacities and the moral bonds between us.

Though we think being scientific means leaving the insights of the humanities and social sciences behind, we forget that not even two hundred years after the Scientific Revolution came the Enlightenment, the 17th century intellectual movement that asserted the natural and inalienable rights to life, liberty, and property, and especially personal autonomy and the capacity for choice. The capacity for choice was seen by Enlightenment thinkers not just to serve individual interests but to be able to produce societies that are more equitable and just, and unbeholden to the unchecked powers of misguided and corrupt leaders.

Unfortunately, the lessons of the Enlightenment didn't stick.

We find ourselves now in desperate need of a 21st century Enlightenment, a renaissance of informed consent and personal choice. Such a renaissance will mean the coexistence of choices that are different from one another, and therefore messy and varied. But, in being so, they will also be perfectly imperfect. They will be, as Friedrich Nietzsche wrote, "human, all too human."

Foxes and Hedgehogs

I did not ask for success; I asked for wonder.

—Abraham Joshua Heschel, *I Asked for Wonder*

I DON'T KNOW.

On a scale of 1 to 10, how squeamish does this sentence make you feel?

If the verbiage floating around social media is any indication, 21st century Canadians score pretty high in terms of our intolerance of uncertainty. In fact, we seem to be drunk on certainty, so completely convinced we are right about what's going on in the Ukraine, why whites are inherently racist, why gender is (or is not) fluid, which politicians will save us and, of course, the truth about COVID-19.

We live fanatically, but possibly unreflectively, by a few simple mantras:

"We're all in this together."
"Trust the experts."
"Follow the science."
(And, if you want to be really safe, "Shut up and don't say anything at all.")

Certainty had clearly taken hold before 2020, with some opinions acknowledged as more socially acceptable, and others more incendiary, than others — supporting Biden/Harris, Green Energy, and women's reproductive rights was much socially safer than the alternatives. But, for some reason, COVID-19 is the topic that really made us 'lean into' certainty. It became the box outside of which we are simply not allowed to think. And the thoughts in that box were expected to be collectivist, uniform, and adopted from so-called 'experts.'

We live our lives today in a thick culture of silence, a certainty culture in which outliers are discouraged, dissenting views are fact-checked into oblivion, and those who question what has been deemed certain are made to run the gauntlet of shame for daring to swim outside the mainstream.

Rather than acknowledge what we don't know, we vilify those who try to penetrate the fortress around our well-guarded beliefs and we even fashion legislation — Bills C-10, C-11, C-14, and C-16 in Canada, for examples — to give the administrative state ever more authority in our lives. We are so certain about what's good and right, on the one hand, and what's dangerous and hateful, on the other, that we confidently entrench that certainty in law.

When was the last time you heard someone say, "I don't know," "I wonder?" When was the last time you were asked a non-rhetorical question? Remember the mantra "There are no stupid questions." Now, all questions are considered stupid and the act of questioning, itself, is a subversive, heretical, even treacherous activity.

I can't help but wonder, why did we become so certainty-obsessed and how did it help to create the culture of silence that allowed the COVID response to unfold as it did? Is our certainty obsession new or have we always been this way? Does certainty serve us? Or is it ultimately too costly?

THE ROAST UPON THE PLATE

In July 2022, I had the pleasure of interviewing former *Global News* control room director Anita Krishna. Our conversation was wide-ranging, but we kept circling back to the theme of uncertainty.

Anita explained that, in the newsroom in the early days of 2020, she started asking questions about COVID. What happened in Wuhan? Why aren't we exploring COVID treatment options? Was there an increase in stillbirths at North Vancouver's Lions Gate Hospital? She said the only response she ever got — which felt more like a recording than a human response — was to be ignored and shut down. The message was that these questions were simply 'off the table.'

Tara Henley used the same language when she left the CBC last year; she said to work at the CBC in the current climate is "to consent to the idea that a growing list of subjects are off the table, that dialogue itself can be harmful. That the big issues of our time are all already settled." To work at the CBC, she said, "is to capitulate to certainty, to shut down critical thinking, to stamp out curiosity."

When did we decide to take questions off the table? What gives this 'table' its epistemic invincibility and why are we so sure about what we are leaving on, and taking off of, it? Are we really so certain that we have all the answers and that the answers we have are the right ones? And, at the risk of mixing metaphors, if asking questions is bad because it rocks the boat, which boat we are rocking and why are we so sure our boat is seaworthy?

Today, we seem to hoard certainty as a stepping stone for status and achievement. The more certain we are, the more we appear right and safe and trustworthy. Our world is bedevilled, as Rebecca Solnit writes, by "a desire to make certain what is uncertain, to know what is unknowable, to turn the flight across the sky into the roast upon the plate."

One thing that strikes me as particularly odd — in a sea of very odd things — is that it is the most complex issue about which we seem to feel most certain.

If we're entitled to feel certain about anything, wouldn't you expect it to be about the little things in life? The coffee mug is where I left it, the gas bill arrives on the 15th, my front door is green. Instead, we seem to reserve certainty for the things which would seem to most resist it: climate change, global politics, COVID policy, the effectiveness of gun control, what it means to be a woman, the war in the Middle East, and the real causes of inflation.

These issues are highly complex. They are multifactorial (involving economics, psychology, epidemiology, warfare, and theology), and are mediated by an unquestioning media and public officials who hardly warrant our trust. The CBC was quite quick, if you remember, to chastise Prime Minister Harper's government for supposedly muzzling the scientists but the same outlet has been silent on the current government's handling of COVID. As our world grows ever larger and more complex — photos from NASA's Webb telescope are showing us new images of galaxies millions of miles away — I find it odd, at the very least, that *this* is the time we pick to be so certain.

WHERE DID OUR CERTAINTY OBSESSION COME FROM?

The insatiable desire to know the unknowable is hardly new. And fear of the unknown, and of unpredictable others, has likely always been with us, whether in relation to the uncertainties we face now, those of the Cold War era, or the fears of prehistoric man struggling for survival.

Perhaps the first recorded story of our certainty obsession — played out to fateful ends — is the Adam and Eve story. The text of Genesis, in which we find the story, is a religious explanation of the origins of mankind. Even if you are not a believer, there is something compelling in the fact that the story has so ably withstood the test of time. It taps into something powerful about human nature, about our weaknesses and our desire to transcend our limitations.

In the Judeo-Christian and Islamic traditions, Adam and Eve are the original human couple, parents of the human race.

According to Genesis 1:1-24, on the sixth day of Creation, God made creatures "in his own image," both "male and female." He placed them in the Garden of Eden, giving them dominion over all other living things. But He commanded: "...you must not eat from the tree of the knowledge of good and evil, for when you eat from it you will certainly die."

Unable to resist the temptation of an evil serpent, Eve ate the forbidden fruit and encouraged Adam to do the same. Immediately aware of their transgression, God doled out their punishment: pain in childbirth (for the woman) and banishment from the garden.

It's interesting that Adam and Eve weren't after good and evil, themselves, but *knowledge* of these. They wanted not to become good but to know all. They wanted epistemic certainty. It's also interesting that, in their attempt to acquire knowledge, we don't find out if they actually got it. We just know there were consequences to the pursuit. Among many things, the Adam and Eve story is a failed quest for certainty. We tried to attain the certainty we were told we couldn't have, and we ended up paying the price for it.

We find cautionary tales about our certainty obsession in pagan tales as well. In one of the speeches about love in Plato's dialogue, *Symposium*, the comic poet Aristophanes tells a fantastical story about the origin of romantic love. Originally, he says, humans were two people conjoined but then became surprisingly strong "and so lofty in their notions" (*Symposium* 190b) that they foolishly tried to become god-like. As a result, Zeus cut them in half each one showing "like a flat-fish the traces of having been sliced in two; and each is ever searching for the tally that will fit him."[16] Our striving for Love is the desire we have to roam the earth searching for our original other half in order to become whole again.

Interestingly, it's not just striving for certainty that yields punishment; questioning certainty can be equally perilous. The Inquisition, for example, is largely a lesson about what happened to those who questioned the orthodoxies of the Catholic Church. In 1633, Galileo Galilei, who dared to suggest heliocentrism — the view that the earth revolves around the sun (and not the sun around the earth) — was tried, found "vehemently suspect of heresy," and was sentenced to house arrest where he remained until his death in 1642, all because the view that we now treat as absolutely certain was then deemed to be unacceptable.

What are the lessons from these certainty stories? Why do they resonate?

One lesson is that they are cautionary tales. They caution us about what happens when you try to attain certainty yourself, or you question the certainty of others. But certainty, history tells us, is often a grand illusion and usually a risky endeavour. Even when functioning in unison (as our most revered social institutions do), humans are not obviously capable of it. And, if you want to face censure or total self-destruction (as Adam and Eve, and many of the tragic Greek heroes, did), being obsessed with certainty is a good way to do it.

When immersed in a crisis, it is easy to feel that our circumstances are unique, that no one has ever suffered as we do, that society has never been so unstable. But I wonder, is this true? Are we now really more certainty-obsessed than ever before? Is there something about the 21st century, with all its technological advances, the exponential growth of AI, and its shifting boundaries between the public and the private that make us more interested in certainty? Or do we cycle through waves of certainty and uncertainty as other scientific, economic, and sociocultural factors change?

STORY AND SCIENCE

One way to answer these questions is to think about story, which might seem like an odd way to begin to answer these questions.

Story developed largely as a way to make sense of the chaotic world around us: our existence and death, how the world was created, and natural phenomena. The ancient Greeks imagined Poseidon striking his trident on the ground to explain earthquakes, and the Hindus envisioned our world as a hemispherical earth supported by elephants standing on the back of a large turtle.

Unknown author - "How the Earth was Regarded in Old times," The Popular Science Monthly, Volume 10, part dated March 1877, p. 544.

Creating stories helps us to manage a complex world that sometimes seems to be spinning out of control, using us as its playthings. Forming beliefs about what underlies these complexities helps to bring some order to our experiences, and an ordered world is a safe world (or so we think).

Religion is one way to do this. The British philosopher Bertrand Russell said, "Religion is based, I think, primarily and mainly on fear. It is partly the terror of the unknown and partly, as I have said, the wish to feel that you have a kind of elder brother who will stand by you in all your troubles and disputes." As a religious person, there is something offensively presumptuous in Russell's statement but I take his general point that religion is at least in part a way of developing narratives with characters and reasons and purposes to help to explain our fears about a world that we struggle to understand.

Science, often prescribed as an antidote to religion, is another way of managing our fears. And this management style is hardly new. The ancient Greeks were obsessed, I think I can fairly say, with the idea that technology (*"technê"*) could offer some control over the chaos of the natural world. The chorus in Sophocles' *Antigone* sings: "Master of cunning he: the savage bull, and the hart, who roams the mountain free, are tamed by his infinite art;" (*Ant.* 1). And in *Prometheus Bound* we are told that navigation tames seas (467-8) and writing allows men to "hold all in memory" (460-61).

Science and technology (including carpentry, warfare, medicine, and navigation), and even art and literature, are all attempts to exert a little control over our vast and complicated world. And some attempts at this are more successful than others. Overall, navigation has made us capable of exploring and transporting people and goods to the farthest corners of our world but even it has its missteps, as the recent Titan submersible implosion reminds us.

Our certainty obsession piqued with the rise of radical skepticism during the Enlightenment (the 17th and 18th centuries in Europe). The most famous doubter of them all, philosopher and mathematician René Descartes, sought to "tear everything down completely and begin again" to find the certain principles with which to build a new system of knowledge. Even for the later Enlightenment thinker and empiricist David Hume, who trusted the senses more than most, certainty is a fool's errand since "all knowledge degenerates into probability" (*Treatise*, 1.4.1.1).

DEFERENCE

Though not new, our certainty obsession has culminated in a more recent shift in Canadian values. The authors of *Searching for Certainty: Inside the New Canadian Mindset* write that the experience of rapid change during the 1990s — economic uncertainty, constitutional battles, and the emergence of new interest groups — made us more self-reliant and more questioning of authority. We became more uncertain, in other words, more discerning, more demanding, and less willing to place our trust in *any* institution — public or private — that had not earned it. We were reassured not by promises, but by performance and transparency. We went through what University of Toronto political scientist Neil Nevitte called a "decline of deference." And, though not directly connected to certainty, our certainty obsession now seems buoyed up by the fact that we claim certainty for ourselves by referring or, more accurately, deferring to experts.

Writing these words gives me chills. Who were *these* Canadians and what happened to them? This is the Canada I remember. This is the one that felt like home. The one with Block Parent signs in every third window. The one with citizens and neighbours in the truest senses of the words.

So I ask, why has deference risen its ugly head once again?

If the 90s' search for certainty was coupled by a trend away from deference, the certainty search of the 21st century seems to depend on it. We are certain not because of our misplaced trust in our own skills but because we outsource our thinking to the experts. And we outsource, it seems, because we are insecure and unconfident in our abilities to navigate our way through complex situations. In addition to this, we hold an oddly unquestioned set of beliefs: government is fundamentally good, the media would never lie to us, and pharmaceutical companies are, first and foremost, philanthropic. Or, perhaps we just believe that enough consistency in the narrative produced by this triad of beliefs makes us able to be reasonably certain about them.

SCIENTIFICALLY CERTAIN

Let's return for a moment to the issue of the infallibility of science from the last essay.

"Trust the science," we are told. What the science supposedly indubitably shows is that there is a climate crisis, that gender is an illusion, and that the COVID response was perfectly "safe and effective." But, nestled in the folds of these deep commitments, is the idea that the mark of an intelligent person, and probably a mature society, is a demonstrated commitment to the *certainty* of these ideas.

Science, we seem to think, has a unique, and maybe infallible, kind of precision. Charitably, this makes a certain kind of sense. It takes time and effort, collectively, to reach a level of scientific certainty. And, those who question what are deemed to be scientific truths after all that collective work are seen as the knuckle-dragging, wet-blanket-throwers who drag society down, keeping us from the progress and the perfection of which we are capable.

We are told, "The science is settled" on all these issues. But is it? "Trust the science." Can we? "Follow the science." Should we?

It isn't even clear to me what we mean by "science" in these oft-repeated mantras. Is the science we are supposed to trust the institution of science (whatever that is), or particular scientists who have been anointed credible representatives of it? Dr. Fauci conflated the two in November 2021 when he tried to defend himself against critics: "They're really criticising science because I represent the science." I'm not so sure.

ESSENTIAL UNCERTAINTY

Though science now has the reputation of being infallible, it is actually the most unlikely of scapegoats for our certainty obsession since, for scientific progress to be possible, certainty must be the exception, not the rule.

One of the basic principles of the scientific method, famously articulated by 20th century philosopher of science Karl Popper, is that any hypothesis must be inherently falsifiable, i.e. potentially disprovable. Some scientific principles make uncertainty explicit, such as Heisenberg's "uncertainty principle," which acknowledges the fundamental limits to accuracy in quantum mechanics, or Gödel's incompleteness theorems, which are concerned with the limits of provability in mathematics.

The evolutionary biologist Heather Heying says that science is precisely about *un*certainty:

> Embracing uncertainty, knowing that you do not know, and that what you think you do know may be wrong—this is foundational to a scientific approach to the world. Over the last decade, and especially since Covid, we have seen an increasing focus on certainty, and on single static solutions to complex problems. Perhaps most alarming of all, those appeals to authority, and to silencing those who disagree, has arrived under the banner of science. #FollowTheScience, we are told, when that has never been how science worked.[17]

American astronomer and astrophysicist Carl Sagan likewise cautions against seeing science as certain:

> Humans may crave absolute certainty; they may aspire to it; they may pretend, as partisans of certain religions do, to have attained it. But the history of science — by far the most successful claim to knowledge accessible to humans — teaches that the most we can hope for is successive improvement in our understanding, learning from our mistakes, an asymptotic approach to the Universe, but with the proviso that absolute certainty will always elude us.[18]

For Sagan, science is marked not by conviction and arrogance but by humanity and humility, the scientist's true virtues. Science always stands at the brink of what is known; we learn from our mistakes, we resist incuriosity, we feel forward for what is possible. And we try always to keep certainty and arrogance in check since they handicap us in science as they do in life.

I have little doubt that humanity's certainty obsession is at the epicentre of the chaos in which we find ourselves. But if science, itself, isn't responsible for it, where does our certainty conviction come from? Part of me wonders if it is due in part to the very simple fact that different people have different ways of thinking about the world, and that these different people dominate at different moments in history.

FOXES AND HEDGEHOGS

"The fox knows many things, but the hedgehog knows one big thing."

The philosopher Isaiah Berlin starts his 1953 essay, "The Hedgehog and the Fox," with this perplexing proverb attributed to the Greek poet Archilochus. Berlin goes on to explain that there are two types of thinkers: hedgehogs, who see the world through the lens of a "single central vision," and foxes, who pursue many different ideas, seizing upon a variety of experiences and explanations simultaneously. Hedgehogs reduce all phenomena to a single organising principle, explaining away messy, inconvenient details. Foxes, on the other hand, have different strategies for different problems; they are more comfortable with diversity, nuance, contradictions, and the grey areas of life. Plato, Dante, and Nietzsche are hedgehogs; Herodotus, Aristotle, and Molière[19] are foxes.

Who are the hedgehogs of our time? And why do we seem to be so outnumbered by them? Are hedgehogs naturally more common or does our education system somehow train the foxes out of us? Is there something about the culture of this historical moment that favours them? Are there any foxes left and, if so, how did they survive? How *will* they survive?

I hope you aren't expecting answers to these questions. I hope you have also figured out by now that I'm not afraid to ask questions for which I don't have answers. But I do have the sense that the way we fundamentally think about the world, whether we approach it with an open or a closed mind, a willingness to question and entertain uncertainty, or a revulsion towards these things, is key to understanding how we have allowed certainty to cripple us.

SWERVING TO AVOID DOUBT

If we cling so tightly to certainty, we must do it for a reason. Perhaps we don't feel like we have the luxury of ambivalence. Perhaps doubt, even just the appearance of it, is too risky in our current environment. Perhaps we fear that giving up the appearance of certainty will expose us to those who will 'pounce' at the first sign of weakness. (In truth, they probably will.)

The easy neurological, and evolutionary biological, answer to why we fear uncertainty is that it threatens our survival. An uncertain environment poses a huge threat. And this isn't just in terms of biological survival (though many are worried, of course, that COVID, or the next novel virus, does pose a serious virological threat). Uncertainties, and acting wrongly on them, could mean the end of financial, relational, and social survival as well.

Uncertainty makes our vulnerability palpable, to ourselves and to others, and so we try to escape it in any way we can. In *The Art of Scientific Investigation,* William Beveridge writes, "Many people will not tolerate a state of doubt, either because they will not endure the mental discomfort of it or because they regard it as evidence of inferiority." We constantly look for the next step, the next rung on the ladder; we reach out desperately for the next swinging rope before letting go of the one we have.

Clearly, a state of doubt imposes a burden. It means there is work to be done, questions to identify, data to sift through. Doubt also means enduring the discomfort of appearing unsure of oneself and, in a social media culture that puts all eyes on us, that may be too great a cost. Certainty gets one off some very burdensome epistemological and social hooks.

But there are costs to this way of living too:

- **Arrogance or excessive pride:** The ancient Greeks called it *hubris* and crafted tragedy after tragedy to warn us of its consequences. We all know what happened to Oedipus when his arrogance propelled him towards his fateful end or

Ajax who thought he could proceed without the help of Zeus. Arrogance, the tragedians teach us, is a short walk from certainty.

- **Inattention**: As soon as we become certain about a belief, we tend to be inattentive to the details that confirm or deny it. We become disinterested in accountability and potentially even deaf to suffering. Trish Wood, who moderated the recent Citizens' Hearing on Canada's COVID-19 response, emphasises the damage done by experts in public health: "Their blinkered approach was inhumane." She says the testimonies of the vaccine-injured were harrowing but predictable but no one was held accountable. All of our institutions, including the media who should be watchdogging them, "have been captured and are complicit." If you are certain you have the answers, then why would you bother attending to details as though you were still on the hunt for answers?

- **Intellectual atrophy**: As soon as we become certain, we no longer need to think of the right questions to ask, or figure out how to work our way out of a problem. We should be unrelenting in our attempt to uncover the origin of COVID-19. But instead, we suppress unwelcome facts and are happy to trade incuriosity for ineptitude. "[T]ruth will come to light," Shakespeare wrote. Well, not if the people don't crave it and have no interest in searching for it.

- **Reductionism**: When we pursue a single narrative, as the hedgehog does, we ignore whatever doesn't neatly fit it. This happens any time people are reduced to numbers (as they were at Auschwitz), or to their skin colour (as they were in the antebellum South), or to their vaccination status (as we all are now). Dehumanization and ignoring complex features of a person go hand in hand, though which comes first isn't always clear.

- **Dampening our spirit**: This is the certainty cost I worry about most. The most interesting people I know are talking about meaning. We are a society, they say, without meaning, without a sense of who we are or what we are doing. We have lost our spirit and our sense of wonder. With all his apparent advantages, the hedgehog is missing one big thing: he has no wonder in his life. He has trained himself away from it. And without wonder, without a healthy dose of "I don't know," what does life feel like? Where does that leave our spirit? How optimistic or excited or invigorated are we able to be?

It is quite possible that certainty has stepped in as a surrogate for something more meaningful that we have lost, some sense of purpose that could fill out our lives more naturally and more fully. Uncertainty makes possible so many beautiful things in life: suspense and wonder and curiosity. Rabbi Abraham Heschel wrote in the preface to his recent book of poems, "I did not ask for success; I asked for wonder." Finding meaning and a sense of identity once they have been lost is no easy task, but identifying them as the *real* source of our certainty obsession is the first step, I believe, in curing ourselves of it.

IT FLIES ON MIGHTY WINGS

I don't know.

This little phrase expresses at once our deepest fears and our greatest powers. As the poet Wislawa Szymborska said in her Nobel acceptance speech, "It's small, but it flies on mighty wings."

I don't know. And that's okay.

In fact, it's unavoidable.

It's imminently scientific.

And it's deeply human.

Today, it's hard not to see uncertainty as a threat and to capitulate, instead, to certainty. Our culture craves instant gratification, simple answers, and obvious (and, ideally, easy) pathways to success. We think uncertainty will put us into an intellectual free fall. But the fact that so many of us have become certainty-obsessed has cost us a lot, especially over the last four years: best practices in medicine and research, accountability in government, transparency in journalism, and civility in relationships. But what it has arguably cost us most is the loss of our own humility and wisdom. As the Greek philosopher Socrates famously quipped in Plato's *Apology*, "I seem, then, in just this little thing to be wiser than this man at any rate, that what I do not know I do not think I know either."[20]

What if we shelved certainty for a while? What if we stopped working so hard to build fortresses around our beliefs and, instead, got comfortable "living the questions?" What if debate in the House of Commons saw more curiosity than declarations? What if our politicians thought to ask us questions from time to time, about what matters most in our lives or what makes us most worried about the future? What if we asked those closest to us about what has happened over the last few years, what it's doing to our children, and what sacrifices we are going to make to take hold of our future?

In times of great uncertainty, the natural instinct is to retreat, to seek the comfortable, the certain, and the anonymity of a crowd. Courage is not the default for most of us. As sociologist Allan Horwitz says, our innate disposition toward self-preservation means that "cowardice is the natural response to danger because humans are instinctively prone to flee from situations that threaten their well-being."[21] Our brains are hardwired to perceive uncertainty as a threat, and so we experience uncertainty as a stress that we need to manage rather than lean into.

Embracing uncertainty in a certainty-obsessed culture will take courage, and courage takes intention and endurance and patience and many other skills that don't offer obvious or immediate payoffs. But the benefits are there.

Psychological studies of humility have surged in the last two decades showing its fascinating link with both cognition and the capacity for prosocial behaviour. Studies show, in particular, that humility is a stronger predictor of performance even than IQ, and that it creates better, more flexible, and empathetic leaders.[22]

Humility also encourages a cluster of moral virtues that bind society together, supporting various social functions and bonds, and opening us up to meaningful connection with others. It helps us to be more tolerant and more empathetic, acknowledging and respecting others at a deeper level. Humility and uncertainty both transcend limitations. They expand our minds by creating spaces that don't need immediate filling, and they lay the groundwork for innovation and progress.

None of this is particularly surprising. To circle back to the topic of meaning, those who are less certain, more open, and more humble find it easier to see their place in relation to something larger, to feel connected to structures bigger than themselves: couples, families, communities, nations, the human race. Humility reminds us that we are members of a species that is far from perfect and that we each have a role to play in how we develop, or regress, together.

o o o

So what can we do, here and now, to embrace uncertainty?

First, please don't let your doubts and the urge to question make you feel small and inferior to those with more apparent confidence. The confidence they emit is likely not their own anyway but rather bought by compliance with a system that demands it. Embracing the uncertainty you naturally have is actually a sign of self-awareness and maturity.

Second, accept that the fox's path is likely to be a lonely one. There won't be many who will applaud your questioning, doubting, and resisting ways. You might lose employment opportunities and important relationships, you might be excluded from social activities, and you might be harassed, online and off. Our current culture is inhospitable to foxes. So if you choose to be one, you need to know the costs. But the freedom it affords will bring you more peace than anything you could achieve by falsely adopting the certainty of the group.

Third, accustom yourself to feeling comfortable with not knowing. Embracing uncertainty is a habit, and it takes intention and time to form positive habits (research suggests somewhere between 18 and 254 days[23]). And remember that it is the skills of the fox, and not the hedgehog, that will be invaluable as our world grows increasingly complex.

If the last four years have taught us anything, it's that the ability to navigate change, to imagine more than one solution to a problem, and to empathise with multiple viewpoints is invaluable. Even if we avoid future pandemics, we won't avoid a world growing ever more complex. And even if science could perfect us in certain ways, by extending our lives and expediting our exploration of the natural world, it wouldn't thereby also make the world a morally simpler place. In fact, it might do the opposite. Crises and disorder create chaos and stress, but they also create opportunities. The question is how to best prepare ourselves to embrace them.

Who will be best equipped for the future? The hedgehog, who sees only one solution to every problem? Or the fox who sees many different solutions? Who will be the most ingenious and adaptive and, ultimately, the most useful and content?

Each of us has a fundamental choice to make moving forward: we can choose to be a hedgehog or we can choose to be a fox.

If we are to save ourselves and our civilization, I believe we need the pendulum to swing in the direction of the foxes.

But it's up to you. What will you choose?

3, 2, 1, TIMBER[24]

Nobody sees it happening, but the architecture of our time
Is becoming the architecture of the next time....

Time slips by; our sorrows do not turn into poems,
And what is invisible stays that way. Desire has fled,

Leaving only a trace of perfume in its wake,
And so many people we loved have gone,

And no voice comes from outer space, from the folds
Of dust and carpets of wind to tell us that this

Is the way it was meant to happen, that if we only knew
How long the ruins would last we would never complain.

—Mark Strand, "The Next Time"

The clock seems to be ticking. Growing disparities in wealth, a housing and gas crisis, transhumanism galloping over the horizon, heroized incivility, and the constant threat of viruses, the 'cures' for which may be worse than the diseases.

Global politics feels eerily apocalyptic these days and, in our own little worlds, many of us are so lost, so unmoored from the comforts of our pre-pandemic lives, we don't know which end is up or what the future will hold.

I wonder, are we falling as Rome did? Is it possible that our civilization is on the verge of collapse? Not imminent collapse, perhaps, but are we taking the initial steps that civilizations before ours took before their eventual downfalls? Will we suffer the fates of the Indus, the Vikings, the Mayans, and the failed dynasties of China?

As a philosopher, to figure out if our civilization is, indeed, on the verge of collapse, I first need to understand what we mean by "civilization" and what it would mean for that kind of thing to collapse.

This is a significant conceptual hurdle. "Civilization" (from the Latin *civitas*, meaning a body of people) was first used by anthropologists to refer to a "society made up of cities" (Mycenae's Pylos, Thebes, and Sparta, for examples). Ancient civilizations were typically non-nomadic settlements with concentrated complexes of persons who divided labour. They had monumental architecture, hierarchical class structures, and significant technological and cultural developments.

But just what is our civilization? There isn't a tidy line between it and the next in the way the Mayans' and the Greeks' coexistence was defined by the ocean between them. Is the concept of Western civilization—rooted in the culture that emerged from the Mediterranean basin over 2,000 years ago—still meaningful, or has globalisation made any distinction between contemporary civilizations meaningless? "I am a citizen of the world," wrote Diogenes in the 4th century B.C.[25] But of course, his world wasn't quite as vast as our own.

Now for the second issue: civilizational collapse. Anthropologists typically define it as a rapid and enduring loss of population, socioeconomic complexity, and identity.

Will we suffer a mass loss of population or socioeconomic complexity? Perhaps. But that isn't what most concerns me. What I really worry about is our loss of identity. I worry that we've lost the plot, as they say, and that with all our focus on the ability of science to save us, we've lost our ideals, our spirit, and our reasons for being. I worry that we are suffering what Betty Friedan called "a slow death of the mind and spirit." I worry that our nihilism, our façadism, and our progressivism are incurring a debt that we may not be able to pay.

As the eminent anthropologist Sir John Glubb wrote, "The life-expectation of a great nation, it appears, commences with a violent, and usually unforeseen, outburst of energy, and ends in a lowering of moral standards, cynicism, pessimism and frivolity."[26]

Think of a civilization as the top step on a staircase, with each stair below having fallen away, its citizens largely ignorant to the technological advances, wars, and political events that got us here. Western civilization today is built largely on the foundational ideals of ancient Greece and Rome that endure long after their physical structures and governments disappeared. But they endure because we find them meaningful. They endure through literature and art and conversation and ritual. They endure in how we marry, how we write about one another, and how we care for our sick and aging.

One lesson history tries to teach us is that civilizations are complex systems—of technology, economics, foreign relations, immunology, and civility—and complex systems regularly give way to failure. The collapse of our civilization is almost certainly inevitable; the only questions are when, why, and what will replace us.

But this brings me to another point. Early in its usage, anthropologists started using "civilization" as a normative term, distinguishing "civilized society" from societies that are tribal or barbaric. Civilized people are sophisticated, noble, and morally good; other people are uncivilized, backward, and vicious even.

But the old distinction between civilization and barbarism has taken on a new form in the 21st century. It is from within our own "civilized" culture that emerges an inversion of the concepts of civility and savagery. It is our professionals, our academics, our political leaders, and our journalists who most ignore the standards of rational discourse, who institutionalize hatred and incite division. Today, it is the elites who are the true barbarians among us.

I can't resist quoting Whitman again who said, "We had best look our times and lands searchingly in the face, like a physician diagnosing some deep disease." If our civilization collapses, it won't be because of an outside attack, like nomads charging in from the desert. It will be because of those among us who, like parasites, are destroying us from within. Our civilization may collapse and it could be due to any number of factors—war, the economy, natural disasters—but the silent killer, the one that may get us in the end, is our own moral catastrophe.

The ultimate problem, therefore, is not interpersonal; it's inner-personal. If our civilization is collapsing, it's because something in each of us is collapsing. And we need to rebuild ourselves first, brick by brick, if we are to have a chance of rebuilding ourselves together.

In The Shadow
Of Oedipus

The greatest griefs are those we cause ourselves.

—Sophocles, *Oedipus Rex*

O ne of the most heart-wrenching things in life is to watch someone make decisions that lead to their own destruction. It's not just watching a person suffer that is hard but watching them make the very choices that create their suffering. And, maybe even worse, realizing that we do this ourselves.

Sophocles' play, *Oedipus Rex*, puts this phenomenon on the stage. It tells the story of Oedipus, a man prophesied from birth to murder his father and marry his mother despite his sincerest attempts to avoid doing either. Sophocles shows us that it is precisely *because* of these attempts that Oedipus is propelled towards his unfortunate end. At the end of the play, Oedipus realizes that his suffering is due to his own choices but, by that point, it is too late to change his course. So ashamed of what he has done, he blinds himself and flees into exile.

In the last essay, I considered whether our civilization is on the verge of collapse. That idea may have struck you as a bit extreme, but even just a cursory look at how we are faring, individually and collectively, suggests that the threads that hold us together are unraveling at a rate outpacing our ability to restitch them. In public and in private, online and in real life, our civil and moral deterioration is affecting how we view persons, how we raise and educate children, to what degree we are willing to sacrifice each other, and how inclined we are even to rewrite history.

In September, 2022, Trish Wood published a disturbingly diagnostic article called, "We Are Living the Fall of Rome (and it's being forced on us as a virtue)" in which she describes us as "a doomed culture pretending not to see its own demise." Wood cites "the normalization of abhorrent behaviour, the race-baiting and censorship, the cruelty and banishment of anyone who objects to the bizarre carnival unfolding in our streets" as evidence of our self-destructive behaviour. Our greed, our collectivism, our relativism, and our nihilism have created fault lines across every facet of life. And COVID seemed only to punctuate our destruction, leaving us with the deep wounds of "pandemic trauma."[27]

Wood isn't wrong. Well beyond anything COVID did to us, or made salient, our society seems to be at a tipping point and it isn't clear that we could shift back to where we were even if we tried. We are a broken people who seem to be breaking a little more every day.

Here, I want to take the thesis of the last essay a step further and explore what might be causing our collapse. Is it a coincidence that we are suffering in so many different areas of life right now? Is it a little misstep on an otherwise progressive path? If we are on the verge of collapse, is it part of the arc of all great civilizations? Or, like Oedipus, do we suffer from some tragic flaw — a collective destructive character trait that we all share — that is responsible for bringing us to this place at this moment in history?

WHAT AILS US?

All tragedies, classical and modern, follow a very specific pattern. There is some central character, the tragic hero, who is reasonably like us but who suffers terribly because of his tragic flaw, the internal imperfection that causes him to damage himself or others. Oedipus' flaw is his excessive pride (or *hubris*) in thinking not only that he could escape his fate but that he alone can save Thebes from the plague placed upon it. It's his pride that drives him to flee his adoptive parents and his pride that causes him to get angry enough to unknowingly kill the man (who turns out to be his father) at the crossroads who will not let him pass. His story moves us because, as Sigmund Freud wrote, "It might have been ours."

One risk of searching for a (collective) tragic flaw to explain our destruction is that it presumes that we are protagonists living out a drama instead of people living in the real world. But our words aren't crafted by playwrights, and our movements aren't staged by directors. We envision our own futures, make our own choices, and act on those choices (or so it seems). And so a question is whether real people, and not just literary characters, can have tragic flaws.

An interesting place to look for an answer is past moments of crisis in which we saw ourselves as, or made ourselves into, protagonists. WWII Britain is a good example, in part because it is relatively recent, and in part because it shares many of the experiences — of fear, social isolation, and an uncertain future — that we are experiencing now. When you read about how the British people rallied together, you can clearly see a sense of agency and moral purpose, and how some of the language used to describe this coming together straddled reality and fiction. A good example is a comment made by John Martin, Winston Churchill's private secretary, to describe how the British people transformed themselves from victims to protagonists: "Brits came to see themselves as protagonists on a vaster scene and as champions of a high and invincible cause, for which the stars in their courses were fighting."[28]

It is also helpful to remember why the Ancient Greeks wrote tragedies in the first place. In the 5th century BC, the Athenians were reeling from decades of war and a deadly plague that killed one quarter of their population.[29] Their lives were framed with uncertainty, loss and grief, and the magnitude of the realization that life is fragile and largely beyond our control. The tragic playwrights — Sophocles, Euripides, and Aeschylus — dramatized the experiences of war and death in order to make some sense of the chaos they caused, to create a semblance of order and reason. Tragic characters were not so much literary inventions as they were reflections of the actual experience of suffering that was all too common in the ancient world. And so, even though the fantastical battles between superhuman and the Olympian gods might seem a long leap from our more mundane lives, the lessons contained within the tragedies might still offer us something relevant and useful.

So I take it as a live and interesting question; are we suffering from a collective tragic flaw? And if so, what could it be? Taking a cue from the tragic playwrights — the Greeks, Shakespeare and even Arthur Miller — the candidates include *hubris* or excessive pride (Oedipus, Achilles, and the *Crucible*'s John Proctor), greed (Macbeth), jealousy (Othello), willful blindness (Gloucester in *King Lear*), and even extreme hesitancy (Hamlet).

In a way, I think we are suffering from all of these, from a complex web of tragic flaws. Our scientism predisposes us to unchecked ambition, our greed makes us excessively self-focused, and our blindness makes us numb to the suffering of others. But when I consider what might be the nexus at which all these flaws intersect, nothing seems to define us at this point in history more than our arrogance; arrogance in thinking we can write perfect essays and curate perfect homes; arrogance in thinking we can eradicate disease and malfunction, and even escape death; arrogance in thinking we can go to the limits of outer space and the depths of the sea without incident.

But our arrogance is precise. It's not just that we think we are better than others, or better than we have ever been. We think we can be superhuman. We think we can become perfect.

THE PERFECT STORM

In an earlier essay, I argued that scientism has captured all sectors of society, powerfully shaping our response to COVID and, quite likely, to future crises. But why did we become doting followers of scientism in the first place?

As a starting point, let's take a look at what was going on in academia in the years leading up to 2020.

For a long time, the implicitly accepted value theories in medical ethics were hedonism (the pursuit of pleasure) and eudaimonism (the pursuit of flourishing via a life of virtue). But, at some point, these theories gradually began to be supplanted by a third contender: moral perfectionism.

You are undoubtedly familiar with perfectionism as a character trait, the pursuit of excessively high personal standards of performance. But moral perfectionism adds the normative component that, to attain the good life, humans *ought* to become perfect in these ways. (Implied is the assumption that it is possible to do so.)

Moral perfectionism is hardly new. In the 4th century BC, Aristotle's moral perfectionism took the form of a virtue theory, claiming that humans have a *telos* (a purpose or goal), which is to attain a state of flourishing or well-being (*eudaemonia*). In simple terms, we need first to develop virtues like courage, justice, and generosity if we are to be capable of living well. Moral perfectionism took on a slightly different form in the 19th century with the utilitarian philosopher John Stuart Mill for whom a fulfilled, virtuous life is cultivated by developing what he called "higher pleasures" (mental pleasures versus pleasures of the body).

But, by the time we got to the 21st century, moral perfectionism had morphed so completely it became unrecognizable. Originally meaning that we could actualize our potential by improving our natures, perfectionism now sets the unattainable goal of *literally* becoming free of defects. The perfectionism of today is the inhuman expectation that our lives are picture-perfect and reel-ready, that we must be superhuman in our physiology, our psychology, our immunity, and even our morality. We curate and style. We prescribe, vaccinate, shame, blame and surgically alter. And we expect as much, or more, from others.

One reason I think our culture was so keen to embrace mass COVID vaccination is that medical intervention, more generally, has taken on an odd sort of social currency. We rack up specialist visits, prescriptions, and surgeries like desirable partners on a dance card. This is a reflection, I think, of the influence of scientism and perfectionism in our lives; it means we are 'on board' with the idea of rooting out and eliminating every last personal flaw and using the latest technology to do so.

This is reflected, I think, in the lack of patience and grace we seem to have for those who choose to forgo whatever medical intervention is deemed able to 'fix' what ails them. I know of a woman who has suffered from depression for as long as anyone can remember. She refuses to take medication or even get a diagnosis. Most of her immediate family has diminishing grace for her simply because they believe she isn't taking advantage of the proposed solutions. She won't do the protocol, so she can "suffer the consequences."

The same intolerance exists for those who resist COVID vaccination. The common response from the devout pro-vaxxers is that we should refuse medical care to those who won't take advantage of the solution offered to them. They won't do the protocol, so they can "suffer the consequences." ("Let them die," as Canada's largest national newspaper recommended.)

It's all so simple. Or is it?

Perfectionism, when it comes to addressing our physical or mental infirmities, is the presumption that leaves no room for questions, nuance, individual differences, reflection, apology, or revision. And it didn't emerge *ex nihilo* in 2020; it started to gain traction decades earlier, as it needed to if it was to mold our COVID response.

PUNCTUATED PERFECTIONISM

There is evidence that this literal and extreme form of perfectionism started to settle into our personalities over 40 years ago. According to a 2019 study,[30] unprecedented numbers of people began to experience self-oriented perfectionism (setting excessively high expectations for oneself), other-oriented perfectionism (doing the same for others), and socially-prescribed perfectionism (believing that one is held to extremely high standards by society) as early as the 1980s. In 2012, the UK Association for Physician Health found that perfectionism is a growing trait among doctors, in particular, who tend to be overly critical of their behaviour, leading to deleterious mental and physical effects.[31]

In his recent book, *The Perfection Trap*, Thomas Curran writes that a perfect storm of globalization and wider environmental factors, including the increased presence of social media in our lives, created favourable conditions for socially-prescribed perfectionism. He writes,

> I found that our world has become increasingly globalised over the last 25 years, with the opening up of borders to trade and employment, and much higher levels of travel,... In the past we were judged more on a local scale, but with the opening of economies what we are seeing is that people are being exposed to these additional global ideals of perfection.

While we might have expected globalization to increase our awareness of others, and therefore our tolerance for diversity, it also provides greater opportunities for comparison. Whether you are making dinner or building a stock portfolio, globalism widened the lens of comparison at a dizzying rate, creating endless opportunities to be made aware of our flaws.

The highly edited and curated aspect of social media exacerbates this effect. Images of strangers at carefully selected moments

of their lives distorts our perceptions of what real life is and what
it can be. The ability to take 50 photos of a single moment and
then delete all but the best creates a false impression of what
life is really like. And the very idea of curation — the process
of editing our lives as though they are to be part of a museum
exhibit — angles us towards perfectionism.

POLITICAL PERFECTIONISM

Another unfortunate effect of perfectionism is that it lends itself
to a certain kind of political organization in which the state has
substantial centralized control over people's lives: statism.

The Enlightenment philosopher Immanuel Kant presciently
argued that a perfectionist society requires government to regulate
human coexistence. This, I suspect, is precisely why we saw so
little resistance to the increasingly rigid COVID regulations which
framed every part of our lives. During COVID, there was no
thought that humans could be left to conscientiously manage
their own interactions, or even that individual physicians could
responsibly guide them. Free choice is irreducibly individualistic,
and therefore messy. It allows that different people with different
values will make different, and therefore non-perfecting, choices.
And so free choice was among the first things to be sacrificed as
perfectionism gained ground in early 2020.

Perfectionism is precisely the value theory one would expect to
predominate in a culture captured by scientism, and it is the one
we find framing every facet of our lives today. Willingly and with
pride, we laid informed consent on the altar of perfectionism not
to protect ourselves, but to *perfect* ourselves. Individual freedom
became the naive idea that we thought 21st century civilization
had matured beyond.

If our tragic flaw is perfectionism, it would explain a lot. It
would explain our comfort with conformity and compliance, since
perfectionism requires us to eliminate the anomalies that detract
from the goal of self-perfection. It would explain our obsession

with Artificial Intelligence, pharmaceutical enhancement, cryogenics, and MAID, and with the general desire to transcend our limitations. It would explain why we thought Zero-COVID — the *perfect* eradication of the virus — was possible. It would explain our interest in curation and our intolerance of the weak, messy parts of life. And it would explain why we favour closure and judgement and the desire to cut people out of our lives with surgical precision rather than working through the tricky parts of a relationship. For better or worse (far worse, I think), our myopic obsession with perfectionism became the monotheism of the 21st century.

PERFECTIONISM AND PANDEMIC PSYCHOLOGY

So, how did the rise of perfectionism in society, generally, culminate in our hyper-perfectionist tendencies during COVID?

A recent study[32] explored the effect of perfectionism on our psychological states during COVID. It showed that perfectionism increased not only the likelihood of experiencing COVID-related stress but also the tendency to conceal health problems in order to be seen by others as perfect. For perfectionists, the possibility of getting sick can be interpreted as an obstacle to achieving flawlessness in various domains of life such as physical appearance, work, or parenting. For the "self-critical perfectionist" and the "narcissist," in particular, personal value is determined largely by external validation, and so virtue-signaling became unsurprisingly prominent during COVID.[33] COVID pushed so unrelentingly on our perfectionist buttons that we tragically drove ourselves into a state of social and personal destruction.

And herein lies the problem. Perfectionism is not just vain or misguided ambition. It reflects a false perception of who we are, a failure to properly "know thyself."[34] It shows that we give ourselves — our strengths and our weaknesses — as little attention as we give others. In setting our sights on perfection, we forget that we aren't capable of it and, more importantly, that the beauty in life doesn't consist of it.

This is one of the greatest lessons the Greek tragedies teach us: that we must accept, and ultimately embrace, the basic uncertainties and imperfections of life. The contemporary philosopher Martha Nussbaum draws on lessons from the Greek play *Hecuba* to make this point:

> The condition of being good is that it should always be possible for you to be morally destroyed by something you couldn't prevent. To be a good human being is to have a kind of openness to the world, an ability to trust uncertain things beyond your own control, that can lead you to be shattered in very extreme circumstances for which you were not to blame. That says something very important about the human condition of the ethical life: that it is based on a trust in the uncertain and on a willingness to be exposed; it's based on being more like a plant than like a jewel, something rather fragile, but whose very particular beauty is inseparable from its fragility.

For Nussbaum, and no doubt for Hecuba herself, the paradox of life is that, while our imperfections are what expose us to suffering, the worst tragedy of all is to try to safeguard ourselves to the point that we can no longer live as the beings we are.

So much of our perfectionism is tied up with hyper-confidence in technology and its ability to suppress the contingencies of life that cause us pain and suffering. Two thousand years ago we invented ploughs, bridles, and hammers to gain some control over the untamed wilderness around us; today, we invent passwords, security systems, and vaccines. But we forget that using technology to improve our lives requires more than mere technical accomplishment; it requires the practical wisdom needed to keep it working for us rather than us becoming enslaved to it.

The very possibility of relationships exposes us to risk. It requires that we trust and accept promises from other people, and even just that they continue living in a state of good health. The other day, I ran into a woman from our local grocery store with whom I have come to be friendly. I remarked on how I hadn't seen her in a while. She said her sister passed away unexpectedly, 2 months after a cancer diagnosis. She also said that, in the midst of mourning this loss, she was also trying to figure out who she was without a sister, without her best friend, navigating a chaotic world as a new and lonely person.

The response to these losses is often to recoil to protect ourselves. When people die, break promises, or in other ways become unreliable, it's natural to want to retreat into the thought "I'll just live on my own, for myself." You see this everywhere today: people severing relationships that become a bit too burdensome, diving into a world of screens in which the characters are more reliable, even if ultimately less fulfilling.

On top of turning away from relationships, we use certainty as an extra layer of protection from risk and uncertainty. The novelist Iris Murdoch hypothesizes that we deal with the uncomfortable uncertainty of life by feigning surety and confidence. Unwilling to fully live into what we are — anxious and uncertain creatures, tender and terrified and fragile throughout so much of life — we train ourselves into being consumed in false certitudes.[35]

Isn't this what we are doing today? We feign certainty about the origins of COVID, the true causes of the Israeli-Palestinian conflict, and the intentions of global political actors. But, when we decide to live this way — perfectly certain and full of pride — we aren't just losing the value that relationships bring to life; we're making a choice to live less humanly since these are the things that make life meaningful.

What it is to have a tragic flaw is not just to make poor life choices. Oedipus didn't just choose poorly; instead, every particular thing he decided to do was ironically and essentially linked to his downfall. It was the self-righteous thought that he was single-handedly ridding Thebes of the source of its plague that propelled him towards his own destruction. Seeing himself as its saviour made him its destroyer.

In a similar way, I believe our obsession with perfectionism is ironically and essentially tied to the fateful choices we made with respect to COVID-19 and in so many other areas of our lives. We are not, it seems, so unlike the tragic characters of literature. By using technology unguided by wisdom to try to control the world around us, we are becoming its slaves. By cancelling others, we are making it impossible to live well, ourselves. And it is our pretence of unity — "We're all in this together," "Do your part" — that is dividing us more than ever. Our tragic flaw, it seems, is ironically and powerfully creating our own destruction.

CATHARSIS

How do we cure ourselves of this tragic flaw?

In literature, tragic flaws get worked out by a specific process called *catharsis*, a process of cleansing or purification in which the tragic emotions — pity and fear — are aroused and then eliminated from the reader's (or viewer's) psyche. Catharsis gets worked out in the theatre much like therapy does in real life; by giving the audience an opportunity to vicariously work through intense emotions and their tragic consequences in the lives of literary characters, emerging somehow rebalanced.[36]

It is not by coincidence that the experience of catharsis is visceral in the way that a good cry takes it out of you, physically. And the origins of the term certainly reflect its connection with physical purgation.

Aristotle typically used *catharsis* in a medical sense, referring to the evacuation of *katamenia* — menstrual fluid — from the body. The Greek word "kathairein" appears even earlier than this, in the works of Homer who used the Semitic word "Qatar" (for "fumigate") to refer to purification rituals. And, of course, the Greeks had the idea of *miasma*, or "blood guilt," which could only be cured by spiritually purifying acts. (The classical example is Orestes whose soul is purified when Apollo douses him with the blood of a suckling pig.) In the Christian tradition, the ritual of drinking Christ's symbolic blood during the communion sacrament helps us to remember his sacrificial death which cleansed us of unrighteousness. The general idea is that our emotions can be whipped up and then released just as we might hydrate, fast, and sweat to purge ourselves of physical toxins.

Catharsis is an integral part of the healing process. Its purpose is to create an awakening, a process of seeing what you have done, who you are, and how your choices impact yourself and others. That awakening is often painful, like the first moments of opening your eyes in the morning or like the prisoners who are blinded by the light as they emerge from Plato's metaphorical cave.[37]

It is not a coincidence, I think, that so many people describe their falling away from the COVID narrative as a kind of "waking up." It's a matter of seeing things in a new light, seeing ducks where you once only saw rabbits. There is a discomfort to it. But there is also eventual relief in that discomfort as the truth starts to come into view.

o o o

If we have a tragic flaw, and if it is perfectionism, then what sort of catharsis might cure us of it? What underlying emotions are involved and how can we whip them up so we can purge ourselves of them?

A good place to start is to think about how collectives — groups of people — tend to respond to emergency or trauma events. 9/11 comes easily to mind. Though it was over 20 years ago now, I remember the days following 9/11 with crystal clarity. I especially remember the way it arrested and solidified us, socially. I was standing in line at a coffee shop on my way to class when I first heard the news. Well before the era of smartphones, everyone stopped to gather in the corner of the shop around a television set that was covering the event. You could hear people breathing, it was so still and quiet. People were looking for some explanation in each other's eyes. Some held each other, most cried.

I was a graduate student at Queen's University in Kingston, Ontario at the time and I remember everyone talking about it when I got to campus. Classes were cancelled, "Closed" signs appeared in store windows. It became the topic of seminars for weeks to come. News coverage overtook regularly scheduled programming for days. I was riveted but exhausted. The media images — of soot-covered firefighters, personal items protruding from the rubble, waves of dust billowing through the streets, stories of children whose parents would never come home and, of course, the searing image of Father Mychal Judge's body being carried out of the rubble.

These images, the ongoing media coverage, the endless conversations and tears and hugs all exhausted us. We were talked out, hugged out, and cried out. In the days, weeks and even months afterwards, I remember feeling physically weak from it all. Maybe we did more than we needed to do but all the sharing was our cathartic release.[38] It was painful but it somehow cleansed us and drew us together.[39]

We engaged in what psychologists call "social sharing" — the tendency to recount and share emotional experiences with others — and it was powerfully cathartic. Psychologist Bernard Rimé found that 80-95% of emotional episodes are shared and that we typically socially share negative emotions after a tragic event in order to understand, to vent, to bond, to seek meaning, or to combat feelings of loneliness.[40]

Sociologist Émile Durkheim explains that it is through sharing that we achieve a reciprocal stimulation of emotions which leads to the strengthening of beliefs, a renewal of trust, strength, and self-confidence, and even increased social integration. It's in sharing that we build a community of those experiencing the same trauma. Research shows that sharing not just the facts of our experiences, but our feelings about them, improves recovery after traumatic events. A 1986 study assigned participants to one of four groups, including a "trauma-combo group," in which participants wrote about not just the facts of their trauma but the emotions surrounding them. Those in the trauma-combo group showed the most emotional healing but also the greatest objective health improvements, including reduction in illness-related doctor's visits.[41]

Now that we've gained some distance from the intensity of the COVID crisis, I am realizing just how radically different our collective response was compared with what I remember about 9/11.

As a traumatic event, shouldn't we have expected a similar pattern of sharing? Where was the deluge of conversations, the emotional meltdowns, the personal stories? Where were all the public hugs and tears?

None of this happened during COVID. We shared the facts but not the experiences. We focused on the statistics, not the stories. There was no COVID "trauma-combo group," no sharing of what it felt like to be terrified of the virus or the government response to it, no coming together over the grief of loved ones dying alone, no sorrow over what it was like to be hated by your fellow citizens or cast out of meaningful social interactions.

In comparison to 9/11, our natural trauma response to COVID was stunted by our deep culture of silence, censorship, and cancellation. The sharing happened in small, isolated groups, and the media coverage was fringe and outlying. But the acknowledged, shared experiences of people living through a global, traumatic event were absent… or silenced.

The fact that we didn't do the emotional work needed for trauma recovery in the natural course of things means we are still saddled with pent-up, tragic emotions. And they aren't likely to dissolve by the mere passage of time. The work will still need to be done, whether it is by us now, or by our children or grandchildren at some point in the future.

So, what do we need to do now? We need families and friends to talk about how the last four years changed them. We need sisters to share their pain and uncertainties. We need Substacks and op-eds and feature articles on the totality of the costs — physical, emotional, economic, and existential — of the pandemic and the pandemic response. We need testimonies and interviews and books of poetry and history to flood the Amazon and *New York Times* bestseller lists. We need all of this to help us make sense of what happened to us. Stories are a balm to our wounds. We need them for our recovery as much as to create an accurate historical record. And until we have them, our emotions will fester a little more each day, with us floating in a kind of COVID purgatory.

LAST THOUGHTS

It's hard to imagine that we are a civilization on the verge of collapse and perhaps even harder still to imagine that we could be the cause of our own destruction. But it's useful to remember that civilizations are not as invincible as we might think. According to British scholar Sir John Bagot Glubb, the average lifespan of civilizations is a mere 336 years.[42] By this measure, we have done quite well, our civilization — with roots in Ancient Greece and the Roman Empire — having lasted much longer than most. It's a sobering fact that every civilization but our own has collapsed. And, for better or for worse, it was the destruction of every prior civilization that allowed for the creation of our own.

But what perplexes me so much about our potential collapse is that we seem to have all the resources to resist it. We have a robust written historical record to show us how perverted leaders, greed, civil war, and the loss of culture and communication destroy us. We are more literate (in a sense) and more technologically advanced than ever, which should have insulated us from some of the common causes of destruction: disease, economic collapse, and global war. You would think that the lessons of history, alone, would have helped us to swerve to avoid our destruction. And yet here we are.

All these resources, yes, but we have little character, little practical wisdom with which to manage them. In the end, we are here because of a tragic flaw that makes us believe in the possibility of living perfectly rather than living well, all the while making us blind to the paradox at the heart of the idea.

Is there an author to our COVID experience, and to our more general destruction? I don't know and I don't think it ultimately matters.

What matters is how we, as individuals, respond. What matters is how much attention we give ourselves and others, whether we ask ourselves the hard questions and root out the character flaws lurking in the darkest corners of our souls. What matters is not that we are characters but that we *have* characters, that we are able to accept responsibility for lives and the choices we make.

It's interesting to me that, even amidst the 'We-don't-need-history' arrogance of the 21st century, the tragic stories of Shakespeare and of Ancient Greece have managed to survive. That, in itself, should give us reason to pause and pay attention. I wonder, why have their themes stood the test of time? Why do they resonate so profoundly? And, most importantly, what are we attempting to teach ourselves through the telling and retelling?

Tragedies are not just stories that help us to make sense of the chaos of the world around us; they are also warnings for the future generations. They are scratchings on the walls of the caves and letters from the past to teach us how to avoid future self-destruction.

Unfortunately, history shows us that we aren't very good at heeding these warnings. It's as though our tragic flaw is standing in the way of seeing the truth about ourselves. We are still lurking in the shadow of Oedipus. And, like Oedipus, it's the things we do to try to avoid our destruction that fate us to play it out. Perhaps we think we are special, or somehow immune. Perhaps we believe we have evolved past the tragic flaws of our ancestors; but we don't see that we are just as weak and willfully blind. Like Oedipus, we are refusing to see and will one day no longer be able to look at ourselves.

I hope I haven't given the impression that working our tragic flaw out of ourselves will be easy or that it will make all of our troubles dissolve in a moment. There's a reason why so many choose willful blindness; it's not sticky. You can go through your day, even a whole life, without raising eyebrows or ringing any socially alarming bells. But confronting our mistakes and working through them is the only possible way forward.

○ ○ ○

Our lives are framed largely by the stories we tell ourselves. And perfectionism is the story we are currently telling. But it's a dangerous and destructive story because it creates "blind spots" that make us unable to see the harm we do. If it's destroying us, then shouldn't we try to write a different story?

A story in which our lives are messy, the future uncertain, and our lives finite.

A story in which we are imperfect beings who listen to each others' stories and offer grace for each other's imperfections.

A story we need to learn to write with new characters we need to learn to be.

A story in which the things that destroy us in one moment can teach and heal us in the next.

In every tragedy, just before climax, there is an eerie calm. The calm of Fall 2023 is deafening. People aren't speaking. Stories aren't being shared. Self-adulation and revisionism abound.

I can't help but wonder, are we experiencing the "falling action" after the climax of our story, or is it still to come? How would we know? Does the tragic hero ever know? The falling action in a play usually includes the character's reaction to the climax, how he copes with the obstacles that brought him to that point, and how he plans to carry on.

How do we plan to carry on? Will we look our mistakes in the face or will we continue to feed the beast that is our obsession with perfectionism? Will we start telling our stories? Will we listen to the stories of others? And, maybe most importantly, will future generations heed our warnings?

Time will tell us. Or, as the tragic playwright Euripides advised, "Time will explain it all."[43]

Angry, Forever?

Be this the whetstone of your sword. Let grief
Convert to anger. Blunt not the heart; enrage it.

—Shakespeare, *MacBeth*

I don't know if you've noticed but people these days are angry. Angry at those who embrace the COVID narrative and those who resist it; angry at politicians for doing whatever it takes to stay in power; angry at public health officials who, instead of showing some humility over the failures of the last four years, maintain that we ought to have masked more and locked down harder; angry at loved ones who continue to betray us or, maybe worst of all, pretend they never did.

And COVID isn't the only source of our anger. It targets those who fly Ukrainian flags (or don't), drive electric vehicles (or won't), move into 15-minute cities (or out of them). Even venturing to the grocery store is an act of bravery where people seem to be looking for a reason to ram their cart into the heels of the person in front of them.

Much of this anger isn't run-of-the-mill indignation. There's an enthusiasm to it. It's a high-impact, visceral kind of disgust bordering on Shakespeare's "tiger-footed rage." And it seems to be less a response to what one does or says than to who one is, a revulsion at another's very being. During the intensity of the COVID crisis, I frequently heard "I can't stand that sort of person," or "Just looking at her makes me furious."

Anger has become such a cultural phenomenon that a Canadian research consulting firm[44] recently launched a "Rage Index," rating our mood about everything from gas prices to rezoning parts of Ontario's Greenbelt. You would think that, coming out of a global crisis, people would feel relieved or even euphoric that it had finally ended. Instead, we seem to be quite happily setting up camp in the untamed wilderness of our more tribal emotions.

Whatever its source, I'm not sure most of us are even aware of how angry we are or what we are angry about, beyond an amorphous weightiness lurking in the background of our daily movements. I sometimes catch myself with a tightened jaw or clenched fist without an obvious cause. The last time I bought bread at our local bakery, the tension was palpable. Bags of sourdough thumped on the counter, angry fingers assaulting the debit machine, doors slamming, voices raised, fur bristled. Why?

Where is all this rage coming from? Are there more reasons to be angry these days? Or is anger just more culturally accepted, or expected? Is it part of being progressive? (If you don't berate the outliers, are you even civilized?) Or have we reached an unexpected and perilous moment of emotional unravelling? And, if so, what (or who) pulled the initial thread?

When I was in graduate school, I read a paper about anger that stopped me in my tracks: "On the Reasons to be Angry Forever." Its author, University of Chicago philosopher Agnes Callard, argues that there are not only reasons to get angry but reasons to *remain* angry, and they are exactly the same reasons we had for getting angry in the first place. Callard describes what she calls "pure anger," a response to the perceived gap between "the way the world is and the way it ought to be."[45] Anger can be a way of taking up the gauntlet, she says, a purposeful form of moral protest aimed at restoring the moral order. It can motivate people to lobby, to vote differently, to stand by unpopular opinions, even to engage in acts of civil disobedience. Joan of Arc's anger inspired her to lead a whole army. Malcolm X said only anger, not tears, can bring political change. And so I wonder, is there a morally pure form of anger that could help us to restore the moral order? Now that we seem to have fallen off the moral 'wagon,' could anger be a way to help us climb back on?

THE FIFTH CIRCLE OF HELL

COVID anger, or "pandemic rage," is hardly a novel topic. Statisticians are tracking it, journalists are exploring its cultural significance, and psychologists, who largely agree that anger is a 'red-flag' alert to a threatening environment, focus on managing anger so it doesn't consume us. (Though the meditation and deep breathing they recommend strike me as weak antidotes to our ire.) Evolutionary biologists say anger has been preserved in us because it is useful, alerting us to interpersonal conflicts of interest so we can bargain more effectively. And psychiatrists typically see anger as a secondary emotion, a response to our fears and anxieties, rather than to a situation itself.

When I am perplexed by something, my classical roots draw me first to the ancients, to see how humans first started to think about it. There, we find two interesting ideas about anger.

One is a close association between anger and madness, a cautionary tale of sorts. The Stoic philosopher Seneca described anger as a temporary madness, likening it to a collapsing building that's reduced to rubble even as it crushes what it falls upon. The other is that anger is a visceral experience, accompanied by changes in the body. The 5th century BC physician Hippocrates' recommendation "to vent your spleen" reflects the ancient idea that there is a physiology to anger — that it changes, or is changed by, the body — an idea that persisted at least until Charles Darwin who claimed that, "without slight flush, acceleration of pulse, or rigidity of muscles – man cannot be said to be angry."

Aristotle took a more calculated view of anger, describing it as a compelling means of persuasion. Anger, he says, is an awakening of the spirited part of the soul, which can be aroused (by orators and playwrights, for example) simply by tapping into the feeling of having been slighted.

Martha Nussbaum elaborates on Aristotle's idea, describing anger as a symptom of ego fragility, a subconscious way to assert power in a world that feels so beyond our control. She says anger involves a "status-injury" or "down-ranking." We anger when we feel that our social position is threatened. We anger at the offender's relative social elevation. We anger at being made a victim. We may even anger as a "Hail Mary" attempt to vindicate ourselves in a world that tries to destroy us.

Perhaps the most well-known literary treatment of anger appears in Dante's *Inferno*, where it occupies the fifth circle of hell, ranking in severity between greed and heresy. Anger shares this circle with sullenness because they are two forms of the same sin: expressed anger is wrath; repressed anger is sullenness. Dante writes that the wrathful attack one another while the sullen stew below the surface, both confined to the muddy swamp Styx (7.109-26) for eternity.

Inferno, Canto 8: Phlegyas ferries Dante and Virgil across the Styx. Engraving from 'The Divine Comedy.' Gustave Doré. 1885.

There is an eerie chaos to the world today, a palpable feeling that we have become unmoored from the basic moral ideals that once bound us together. We are not, it seems, so unlike the enraged souls in Styx condemned to torture each another until they are both devoured. That was hell, literally. But, in many respects, it's where we find ourselves today.

The thing about hell (or *one* of the things about it) is that it is a place of brokenness and separation; broken souls separated from life, from God, and from each other. What happened to us during the pandemic bears an eerie resemblance to this place; it separated us in ways we couldn't imagine and created its own personal hell for so many who found themselves jobless, unfriended, broke, or disenchanted with others and with life.

Anger can be destructive, no doubt. And sometimes its destruction is perfect and permanent. But the realist in me thinks that, whatever its disvalue, our anger isn't going anywhere anytime soon and we would do well to figure out how to channel it into something useful. To understand what this might look like, I want to begin by looking at how anger is related to other moral virtues, courage in particular, to see whether it is always destructive, or sometimes useful and justified.

FUEL FOR OUR COURAGE

Angry people today are often portrayed as cowards. They are chastised for not letting things go, for not growing up, for refusing to comply and make the needed sacrifices during a crisis. But while anger can sometimes be a way to dodge other, more difficult-to-process emotions, research suggests that it can also be a catalyst for some of the moral virtues, courage in particular.

In a 2022 behavioural study,[46] researchers explored the connection between anger and moral courage. While participants were supposedly waiting for the study to start, they overheard two experimenters plan, and then, execute the embezzlement of money from the project fund. (The embezzlement was staged.)

The participants had various opportunities to intervene, including directly confronting the experimenters, involving a fellow participant, or reporting to a superior. Depending on your perspective of the events of the last few years, you may or may not be surprised to learn that only 27% of participants intervened. (Other experiments, including the Milgram experiment, confirm the natural human inclination towards passivity). Interestingly, researchers found that the more an individual reported feeling angry, the more likely they were to intervene, showing that anger can serve as an important catalyst for moral courage.

There were a lot of reasons to be angry over the last four years. The vaccinated were angry at the unvaccinated for what they saw as irresponsible behaviour. The unvaccinated were angry at those who fuelled what they took to be a misleading narrative. Even now, complicity and inauthentic forms of redress — gaslit justifications, weak contrition, and empty apologies — are ubiquitous. Those asking for "COVID Amnesty," a Prime Minister claiming he never forced anyone to get vaccinated, the friends who shut us out, and of course Anthony Fauci denying in 2022 that he recommended "shutting everything down" (even though he said in an interview in October 2020 that he told President Trump to "shut the country down"). The list goes on and on.

Shouldn't these things enrage us? Shouldn't they leave us with exactly the same reasons to remain angry that we had to get angry in the first place? And wouldn't it actually be cowardly to abandon your anger just because others expect it or because you expected it eventually to give way to tamer emotions?

Though it might be hard to reconcile the idea of morally pure anger with a picture of the virtuous person as rational and even-keeled, being good doesn't necessarily mean being indifferent. Sometimes anger is justified, and sometimes it is exactly what injustice demands. Having a "good temper" doesn't mean being apathetic; it means we need to ensure that our anger is dispensed appropriately. And I think we need to consider that it may only be anger's intensity, its incandescence, that can do certain kinds of moral work, energizing us to fix what cool-headed indignation cannot.

A CAVEAT

However we try to justify it, anger is a dicey business. And we have long known it. There are thirteen different words for "anger" in Homer, one of them being the special subject of the *Iliad,* a cautionary tale about characters so angry they crossed the Trojan plain to slaughter one another. The Greeks and Romans knew that anger can be a social poison, an anathema to healthy public life, making us say and do things that can't be undone. I'm sure you can easily think of examples in your own life in which rage and vindictiveness operated like a positive feedback system, feeding the beasts that create them.

And it's important to remember that anger can destroy not only its perpetrators but its victims as well. Being slighted, stigmatized, and oppressed — some of the common effects of anger — can create enduring moral wounds. It can make you bitter, envious, and myopic about the role you played in creating your own circumstances, and unconfident about the effectiveness of standing up for yourself. It makes you tired in your soul, nurturing a 'why-bother,' self-affirming attitude. Just because anger is sometimes justified doesn't mean there aren't deep moral costs.

It's also important to remember that, useful though it may be, anger is a finite resource. It is reactionary and naturally wanes over time. Intense anger cannot be maintained indefinitely if only because we don't possess an infinite resource of the hormones and neurotransmitters that support it (epinephrine, norepinephrine, and cortisol, to name a few). The intensity of these emotions makes you battle-weary and "burned-out," the signs of a body exhausted of the chemicals needed to support those emotions. Rage is exhausting, possible to sustain for a time maybe, but hard to rely on as a long-term motivator and harder still to keep confined to one area of your life. I sometimes worry that the rage

I allow to fuel the public work I do will seep into the private areas of life where it could undermine the softness I need to be a good friend, spouse, and mother. How careful we need to be not to let the anger we harness for important moral work turn us into angry people, more generally.

IT'S PERSONAL

So what is the real injury we have done to each other with our anger?

One thing I think that the angered and the victims of anger can agree on is that the pain and destruction our anger causes is deeply personal. Anger is a kind of moral looking past or looking over. As Nussbaum says, anger is a voluntary failure to take another seriously, treating them as having so little worth they don't even deserve acknowledgement. Our cancel culture, which not only tolerates but celebrates cancellation, takes this to the extreme. Managing our disagreements by excising and silencing others, thinking of ourselves as so morally superior that our indignation is justified, ultimately dehumanizes us all.

Isn't this the essence of the pain felt by being the victims of anger today? It's not the particular things others say or do to us, but the feeling that we are being dismissed, that we aren't seen as persons with unique histories and feelings and reasons for what we believe. The default reaction first to reference fact-checks in conversations with loved ones, as opposed to asking questions and listening for answers, shows that we are routinely guilty of overlooking, and devaluing, the people in our lives.

But all is not lost. There is a positive side to the deeply personal aspect of anger. The intensity of our anger, and the personal ways in which we feel it, shows that we are deeply social beings, and that the more angry we get, the more we feel something valuable slipping away. It shows us just how perilous social life can be, and that we are not wholly self-sufficient, capable of fully flourishing without one another. Relying on others is a risky business, leaving us sometimes wondering if it's a risk worth taking. And it makes plain the harrowing truth that being seriously wounded in our most intimate relationships is always a possibility.

It's natural to experience these wounds as a deep loss. The loss of being loved and cared for, yes, but also the loss of being someone who loves, who cares for others, and who can experience the choreography of a shared life. When it comes to couples whose relationships didn't survive COVID, they didn't just suffer the loss of a partner but loss of who they were in a partnership.

Payback is especially attractive when one suffers in these ways because retribution feels like a satisfying way of returning in kind the deeply personal ways we were wounded. It is tempting to focus on the past where we understood who we were, and where our contributions felt valuable. That can be much easier than recreating ourselves for an uncertain future. And so it is tempting to make others suffer in the present for what they did in the past.

But there is a problem with using anger to try to correct the past in this way: the past, however vibrant and painful its events can feel in the moment, cannot be changed. And trying to change it is a fool's errand. The past is set. There are no resources there to satisfy our need for justice. Retribution bypasses what we really need when we are angry: an acknowledgement that we have been wronged, and a recognition that the other's words and actions caused pain; they had a victim.

This is why people — whether it be politicians or loved ones — asking for amnesty is so painful; because it bypasses the acknowledgement that we were hurt in the deepest ways possible. What victims of injustice need is not retribution but acknowledgement and the recovery of what never should have been lost.

But what do you do when what was lost is irrecoverable, a reputation or a child's life? What do you do when you know there will never be an apology? We must find a way to move on even without it. If we dwell on the loss, there's no healing and no moving forward.

A wise friend recently reminded me that wrongdoing that happens to us is often not about us. As she elegantly said, "the

wounds people inflict can come flying out through the violent
vortex of their own dysfunction and hit us like shrapnel." And so
our wounds become the byproduct of their wounds. I'm not sure
this lessens the intensity of the wound, itself, but realizing that the
injury is not as personal as it might have been helps us to move
forward. We can feel sorry for the broken and terrified person
our perpetrators are while at the same time carefully holding the
memory of the wrong they did to us in our pocket as a reminder
and a warning.

Sometimes there is no possibility of acknowledgement, no hope
for apology. And sometimes forgiveness is a tall order. The only
way forward might be to honour our injury by remembering the
harm while letting go of the idea that those who harmed us will
be part of the story of our healing.

IN SEARCH OF A CURE

If Seneca was right that anger is madness in need of a cure, what
could cure us of the pandemic of rage we find ourselves in today?
How do we isolate and develop the morally pure and purposeful
form of anger, and purge the more destructive forms? How do
we catalyze the wanton anger that consumed us during COVID
into something that has a hope of addressing the problems that
put us there?

As it often does, history offers some suggestions, some more
promising than others. Before he became emperor, Augustus was
tutored by the Stoic Athenodorus Cananites who offered him
the following advice, "Whenever you get angry, Caesar, do not
say or do anything before repeating to yourself the twenty-four
letters of the alphabet."

The idea that reciting our ABCs will quell our 21st century
rage is a bit laughable but perhaps we have our own versions of
Athenodorus' advice that are equally ineffective. Nasty Tweets,
honking at a stranger in the parking lot and other micro-out-
bursts of aggression might feel like satisfying releases of pent-up

frustration. Doom-scrolling and binge-shopping might feel like apt antidotes for our rage. But neither address the true cause of our anger.

So what *could* cure us?

The ego isn't a bad place to start. I said earlier that Nussbaum relates anger to ego, describing it as a natural response to social downgrading, or to the loss of reputation or power. Decades of research confirms her suggestion. It shows that we tend to rate ourselves more highly compared to others on a variety of positive measures, including intelligence, ambition, and friendliness (a finding referred to as the "self-enhancement effect") but that we do so most profoundly when it comes to moral attributes; we typically believe that we are more just and honest, and generally more virtuous than other people.[47] We tend to believe the best about ourselves and the worst about others; the injustice can't be *my* doing as I am clearly the more aware, socially conscious person. So it wouldn't be surprising if Nussbaum is right that anger is rooted in egocentricity.

Anger that is rooted in the ego is personal in nature and more likely to be looking for a scapegoat to appease its pain and suffering. Ramming the shopping cart into a fellow shopper's heels feels good. Or it seems to. Your anger, at least gets a point by making someone else hurt.

The morally pure form of anger, on the other hand, seeks true justice. It saves its energy not for revenge but for peace. And it knows that taking others down, even enemies, only compounds the injury of an already injured world. Ego-based anger is short-sighted and destructive. Righteous anger, on the other hand, turns a cheek, but keeps its eyes open in the process. It plays the long game, moving forward with clarity and calculation, rather than selling out to cheap and momentary revenge.

There are a lot of reasons not to embrace victimhood. Dwelling too long on the idea that we are victims makes the story about us. It gives our ego power. Remember the point above about perpetrator harms being more about the perpetrator than the victim. If you remove yourself as the subject of the story, it's easier to realize that the harm wasn't personal. And there's something about that which dampens the pain a little.

Our egos have been profoundly affected over the last four years. Being unable to work, travel, or consent, and being disrespected, silenced and shut out are pretty extreme forms of social downgrading. It's not at all surprising, or unreasonable, that they would anger us.

But we need to be careful with ego. Even if it is sometimes a useful defence against being downgraded, self-righteousness can be destructive because it intensifies the distance between ourselves and others, reduces our willingness to cooperate and compromise, and can lead to intolerance or even violence.

No new information here. We know from Sophocles what happens to those whose egos run amok (think of the consequences of Oedipus' excessive pride and Creon's stubbornness). This is at least in part why the tragedians crafted theatric opportunities for catharsis, a kind of moral exorcism to purge ourselves of destructive emotions just as we might cleanse ourselves of a physical toxin.

Are we in need of a moral catharsis today? If so, what would this look like? What could we do to identify and purge ourselves of our pent-up anger and amorphous frustration?

Unfortunately, true catharsis isn't easy to come by. It certainly isn't achieved by snide comments, angry tweets, and other acts of passive aggression, as effective as these sometimes feel. And catharsis isn't just a matter of releasing anger. It requires confronting the flaws that caused us to make the choices that ultimately led to our tragic destruction. True catharsis requires self-awareness and self-knowledge, and creating those can be the hardest, most painful work of all.

But isn't this exactly what we need today? We need to look our mistakes in the face, and acknowledge our role in the suffering of ourselves and others. We need to come face-to-face with the harm done even by our acts of compliance and acquiescence that, at the time, seemed so harmless. We need to atone for our willful blindness and turning our backs on the people and causes that needed us most. And we need to confront the consequences of the vacant defence, "I was just following orders." True catharsis requires much soul-searching and atonement, and I worry that this might be too much to expect at a time when introspection is so unfashionable.

GRIEF CONVERSIONS

Being pure in purpose doesn't mean anger will always be pure in experience. And just because anger can be productive doesn't mean it can correct for all past wrongs. Some parts of our broken world are beyond repair: the child who dies because of bad government policy, the social stunting from unnecessary lockdowns, time and opportunities lost, and systemic mistrust built up over years of gaslighting and betrayal.

The moral work required to stand up for what one believes in has left many feeling burnt out, lonely, and unsure of how to carry on. The rationally angered might feel foolish that their initial hope was misplaced, or they might grieve the loss of what they might have been in a more just world. I sometimes feel resentful that a more peaceful and innocent life has been stolen from us. And I resent the fact that it is those who have caused the most harm, who have the 'dirtiest hands,' who are the least likely to do this work.

So, what do we do with our feelings about the injustices that can't be fixed? What does virtue allow us to do, require us to do, next?

The typical, and some say appropriate, emotional response to facts that are regrettable but unchangeable is grief. Grief at the loss of what was, of who one was, or of what might have been. And so perhaps it isn't surprising that the words for "anger" and "grief" share a common origin (the Old Norse root of anger, "angr," means "to grieve or distress," and "Angrboda," a supernatural being in Norse mythology, means "The one who brings grief").

If Callard is right, that "there are not only reasons to get angry but reasons to *remain* angry, and they are exactly the same reasons we had for getting angry in the first place," then anger can be a way to transform our grief into something productive. As *MacBeth*'s Malcolm suggests, "Let grief convert to anger; blunt not the heart, enrage it." But not all injustices can be fixed by getting up on our white horse and riding out into our broken world to fix them. Morally pure anger, as productive as it can be, can create a false promise of agency in a world that offers increasingly less control over every facet of life. When anger has no productive outlet, when past wrongs cannot be fixed, then anger may have nothing left to do but convert to grief. And we can grieve and honour our losses as peacefully and reverently in measure with what they deserve.

∘ ∘ ∘

Let's end by returning to Callard's question: Should we stay angry forever?

Possibly. But, unlike those who joyously settle into their contempt, the rationally angered won't celebrate others' hardships. They won't cancel, berate, mock or shame, and they certainly won't dance on graves.

But they also won't forget.

To be clear, I am not advocating for wanton terrorism, for burning down buildings or shutting down cities to bring attention to injustice. Even morally pure anger doesn't justify frivolous destruction. But as long as we are clear about what should come 'out' of our anger, it can be an ethical weapon as precise as a surgical scalpel.

Also, the reality of our world is that slow, incremental change to a broken system is not always enough. The fractured institutions of today — health care, government, media, education — demand wholesale change. When we are told that only certain ways of living are valid, and only certain people matter, namely those who follow a particular narrative and endorse a broken system, it is time to rebuild that system. Major societal change often comes about only when attempts at gentle correction toward a more reasonable course have proven futile. Rosa Parks sat down on the bus after two centuries of failed attempts to fight segregation.

Sometimes the realities of our world stretch our humanity too far. The prevalence of pent-up frustration today might be a testament to the gap we perceive between where we are and where we might have been. If so, we need to see that for what it is. We need to take up the gauntlet, and prune our anger into something that has a chance of repairing our moral injury so we are better equipped for the future.

Please don't think that, to be good, you need to be quiet and agreeable and complacent. And please don't think that any of this will be easy. But it will be preferable to the personal destruction and social division created by festering, unacknowledged anger. To that end, let me leave you with the words of the classicist William Arrowsmith who writes, in his commentary on *Hecuba*, about resisting madness in the face the world's injustice:

> Man continues to demand justice and an order with which he can live...and without the visibility of such order and justice, he forfeits his humanity, destroyed by the hideous gap between his illusion and the intolerable reality.

Indeed.

Hope And Moral Repair

We've got to be as clear-headed about human beings as possible, because we are still each other's only hope.

—James Baldwin, *A Rap on Race*

L et's begin with a story I received from a friend, who I'll call "Beth." I asked how she is feeling now that we have emerged from the intensity of the COVID crisis. This is what she wrote. She called her story "Mourning."

In fall of 2021, I issued an invitation to a friend to set up a play date between our seven-year-old daughters. We were family friends. Our children had grown up together, and hers was a perspective that I respected and appreciated. At the time, my family had recently recovered from Covid and I was hoping to reconnect. The reply I got was this: "We are choosing not to see the children of parents who have chosen not to be vaccinated. Maybe I will feel differently later."

I know now and knew then that it was an extraordinary moment of fear and endeavour to at least understand her decision at that time, but the fact remains, my children were overtly "othered" and excluded by someone I knew and valued. That was an unprecedented and pivotal moment for me and one I am still processing. Of course, this came at a time when my children were also excluded from sports and restaurants and birthday parties and family events—all of which were painfully unjust and, if I'm honest, I have still not come to terms with. But, of all the things that transpired at that time, the one that kept me up at night is that message from my friend.

Unfortunately, mine is not an extraordinary story and not the worst of the 'othering' and excluding that ran rampant at that time. There are those that lost jobs, intimate relationships, businesses, endured financial hardship, faced coercion and injury, and those whose reputations were scourged. The ugly list goes on and on.

The loss of any of these things, never mind several of them, has myself and others still in a state of evolving mourning, and, in our ways, we have moved on, but some of it still lingers. The most poignant and lasting mourning seems to be that of our faith in the goodness of human nature.

When the World Health Organization declared a pandemic on March 11, 2020, our lives changed in an instant. Apart from anything it did to our bodies, our economy, or our ways of creating and enforcing social policy, we started to organize ourselves into adversaries on one side or the other of a high-stakes civil war. We quickly learned how to identify the enemy, and we complied and virtue-signalled our way into the social positions we thought would best protect us.

We were hurt by being lied to, of course, and by being silenced and shut out. But the far deeper wounds are the ones done to our capacities as moral beings — our ability to see and empathize with each other, to think critically about how to treat each other, to act with confidence, courage, and integrity, and to approach the future and each other with hope. It became clear, as each day passed, how toughening ourselves for this war created a kind of moral scar tissue in the way courser, less sensitive skin replaces normal skin after physical injury.

Here, I want to focus on how moral injury — a specific kind of trauma that arises when people face situations that deeply violate their conscience or threaten their core moral values — became the invisible epidemic of the COVID era, how we became each others' victims, and how we might begin to repair these injuries.

WHAT IS MORAL INJURY?

Back to Beth for a minute.

Beth's story is remarkable but not, unfortunately, at all uncommon. In fact, it is barely distinguishable from those contained in thousands of emails I have received from people, near and far, with messages of loss, desperation, support, even hope. But its ubiquitousness doesn't humanize it. It's a story of exclusion and abandonment. And it's a story of how all these things changed her to her core.

Beth has been devoted to the freedom cause from the start, working with a prominent Canadian medical freedom organization for almost three years. We live provinces apart and have never met but I would say we have become close. She is a mother who had to navigate her children's experiences through the school system, a writer who tries to organize, in words, the harrowing journey we are on, and a friend who knows the wounds of betrayal.

Beth's story made me think about how the challenges of the last four years have shaped us as moral beings. Believing we were treated with lower priority because of our vaccine status, being told that our choices are unacceptable, and generally being hated, ignored, and abandoned don't just impact us psychologically; they wound us, morally. Think of what it does to your ability to stand up for yourself when you are repeatedly shut down, or your ability to empathize when you realize that your loved ones would be quite happy to move on without you. What reasons do you have to speak again, to trust, or to have faith in humanity? What reasons could you have?

I noticed some significant interior juggling going on in myself over the last four years. Losing professional relationships I had built over 20 years, being shamed by people I deeply respected, and feeling a growing lack of kinship with fellow citizens who felt more like strangers than neighbours all 'left a mark.'

These days, though no less committed to my beliefs, I feel morally weary. I find it harder than I did to be trusting and tolerant. I have, more than once, walked out of a store because the shopkeeper invaded my privacy a little too much. I have lost the patience to draw clear but reasonable boundaries. My moral resources have been worn down or at least marshalled for other, more important tasks, and when I feel them being called upon for something trivial, I resent it and retreat. My default response these days is to recoil to a safe space. If tolerance is a virtue, then in some ways I have become less virtuous. In other ways, I am much braver but that has created a certain hardening as well. When I joined the organization I work for now, I told the founder that I was entering into it in a state of distrust not because of anything he did that warranted it but simply because that has become my moral reflex.

Ethicists refer to these ways of being harmed as "moral injury." The term emerged in the context of studying soldiers returning from war who bore the deep psychological scars of conflict, often called "the war after the war." But it came to be used more broadly to capture the moral effects of other traumatic events including rape, torture, and genocide. Though the idea is not new — Plato discussed the harmful effects of acting unjustly on the soul in the 5th c. BC[48] — it was first officially defined by clinical psychiatrist Jonathan Shay in 1994[49] as the moral effects of a "betrayal of 'what's right'." Moral injury is a wound to our conscience or moral compass when we witness, perpetrate, or fail to prevent acts that transgress our moral values. It is a "a deep soul wound" that erodes our character and our relationship to the greater moral community.[50]

Moral injury is not just egregious harm; it is *the way* in which a person is harmed that matters. It's not just being unseen but the way being unseen converts to feelings of shame, self-doubt, and cynicism, and how these create new topographies of character, transforming who we are as moral beings and our ability to do what is right in the future.

One of the reasons moral injuries are so personal is that they denigrate the moral standing of the victim while simultaneously elevating the moral standing of the perpetrator. We don't just suffer but we have to witness the elevation of the person who hurt us *because* they hurt us. When Beth's friend shamed her, her friend not only excluded her from a social activity; she did it (consciously or not) to demonstrate her moral superiority, her solidarity with the pure and inviolate.

Think of all the ways we have denigrated each other over the last four years, how in big and little ways we diminished each other in order to aggrandize ourselves: by failing to listen, by shunning and shaming, by blaming and casting out, by calling a loved one "crazy," "fringe" or "conspiratorial."

At the end of her story, Beth elaborates on the hurt she felt that is a sign of her moral injury:

> *It wasn't the loss of a job, it was that our colleagues turned their backs. It wasn't my son being excluded from soccer, it was my sister insisting it was justified, and the familiar face who demanded medical information at the door of the local sports centre. It wasn't a lone politician calling names, it was our institutions and neighbours parroting the same, dehumanizing segments of the population. And, quite frankly, it was the people that support and continue to support those who would strip us of our humanity in divisive rhetoric.*

It was Christmas, weddings, family members, classmates, and communities. The things closest to our humanity. These things are still raw, the things we mourn to this day--the knowledge that when the cards were down, our institutions, our colleagues, and our friends would abandon reason and principle and the heart of human connection and cast us aside directly.

"We are choosing not to see the children of parents who have chosen not to be vaccinated."… wrote Beth of her friend's justification for canceling their playdate.

"choosing not to see…"

This short, seemingly harmless justification is a token of the type of cancellation that became the norm over the last four years. Even the strongest bonds going into 2020 — those of long-time colleagues, dearest friends, parents and children — were dexterously severed with the unquestionable, seemingly innocuous justification that we were simply "keeping people safe."

WHAT DID WE EXPECT?

To understand why we are so able to cause these deep moral wounds, it is helpful first to understand that morality is, at its core, relational, whether you are dealing with the relationship you have with another person, with society generally, or even just with yourself. As ethicist Margaret Urban Walker explains, "Morality is the study of us as beings capable of entering into, sustaining, damaging, and repairing such relations."[51]

It is also helpful to understand the normative expectations we have that make relationships possible in the first place. Normative expectations are, broadly speaking, expectations about what people *will* do combined with expectations about what they *should* do. When we place trust in our doctor, for example, we have a predictive expectation that he has the skills to protect us (to the degree that is possible) and the normative expectation that he *should* do so. Betraying this trust by failing to disclose information about a treatment's possible harm would breach this expectation. We have a similar expectation that things we share in confidence with friends will not be traded for any amount of social currency, and that we will treat each other with respect through our differences.

What makes relationships possible is that we set the right expectations, and that we trust ourselves and others to honour them. These expectations set the parameters for acceptable behaviour, and keep us responsive and responsible to each other. It is precisely these expectations that the COVID narrative demanded we breach.

Much has been written about the harm compliant health care workers did during COVID and also about the psychological costs of doing what one believes to be harmful. I don't think it would be an overstatement to say that, in Canada today, nearly every health care professional who is still employed breached their obligations to patients and colleagues because of what the COVID response required of them. To put it in simple, albeit horrifying, terms, if your doctor still has his or her license, then you are likely being treated by someone who has egregiously broken the Hippocratic Oath and every major modern bioethics and professional code of practice.

I often think of the doctors and nurses who were ironically and cruelly asked to spend their days doing the very things that drew them to their profession in the first place. And I think of the costs to dissenting physicians like Dr. Patrick Phillips and Dr. Crystal Luchkiw: shaming, the loss of income and professional relationships, the inability to practice, etc. The week I am writing this chapter, Dr. Mark Trozzi is set to have his disciplinary hearing with the Ontario College of Physicians and Surgeons, and is quite likely to lose his licence to practice medicine. But, as unjust as these costs are, they pale in comparison to the loss of integrity that comes from doing what you believe to be wrong. Drs Phillip and Luchkiw and Trozzi can, at the very least, lie their heads on their pillows at night knowing that they did only what their consciences would allow.

It's helpful to remember that being pressured to do what we know to be wrong and being prevented from doing what we know to be right morally injures not just the victim but the perpetrator as well. Betraying a loved one doesn't just hurt her; it also means the loss, to you, of the person you were in the relationship with, and it can turn you into a morally callous person, more generally.

Interestingly, we don't always know what our normative expectations of others are until they are violated. We may not have realized how important it is to be able to trust a doctor until that trust was broken, or how much we expected our friends to be loyal until they betrayed us. A key part of the COVID narrative is that friendship, marriage, sisterhood no longer matter if your loved one's behaviour is 'unacceptable.' And if it is, then dissolving these relationships is morally justified, even heroic.

CREATIVITY AND OPENNESS

One of the deepest moral injuries we experienced over the last four years was to our capacities for creativity and openness. To illustrate this point, consider this story a close friend relayed to me about a discussion she had with her husband over trying to decide what book to listen to on a road trip. She writes:

> I suggested a book on musical creativity — and pre-pandemic he may have wanted to hear more than one. But, post-pandemic he's not up for the challenges the book might inspire. He wants easy listening, comedy, simple ideas. He said that he is recognizing in himself that the pandemic stifled his ability for openness to novel thoughts and creativity.

You might think that the loss of creativity and openness, though regrettable, have little to do with who we are as moral beings. But they are surprisingly relevant. Creativity makes possible "moral imagination," helping us to creatively imagine the full range of options while making moral decisions and to think about what affects our actions might have on other people. It also helps us to imagine what a more just world looks like and to envision how we might bring it about. And it helps us to be empathetic. To imagine is to form a mental image of what doesn't exist. It is to believe, to picture, to dream. It is both idea and ideal. As the poet Percy Shelley wrote, "The great instrument of moral good is the imagination."

I suspect that my own loss of tolerance and patience has a loss of creativity and openness at its core. Creativity takes energy and openness takes a certain amount of optimism. In some ways, it's easier just to defect from the moral work relationships require than it is to figure out how to remain open in a hostile environment. I recently went on a little writing trip to an area with a small island surrounded by rocky shoals and inhabited only by a few residents and a sheep farm. I imagined, for a moment, migrating there, the isolation and the unnavigable shoals protecting me from the intrusions of the world.

It is understandable that I would want to just give up on people these days. It feels safer, less burdensome somehow. But giving up isn't really an option because it makes us lose out not only on the value relationships bring to our lives but on our ability to be fit for them. It is to give up on our own humanity. As James Baldwin said in his conversation on race with Margaret Mead, "We've got to be as clear-headed about human beings as possible, because we are still each other's only hope."[52]

DOUBLE TRAUMA

One of the things that struck me most about the last few years, as a former ethics professor, is just how different ethics is in practice from teaching it in the classroom or reading about it in an academic journal. It is so much messier, and so much more dependent on emotions and various pressures related to survival than I ever realized.

Every speech I've given over the last few years, the moment when the tears well up is when I start thinking about our children. Children who are 6 years old now who lost an unfathomable half of their lives due to COVID, children who were born into a world of masks and mandates, children who lost out on the opportunity to experience normal social interactions. It will no doubt be a very long time before we know what the true costs of those losses will be. It has been said that children are resilient but, of course, innocence is only so buoyant. We will never know what these childhoods would have been like, or what their futures could have been, or how our world will change on account of these things, if the last four years had been different. And it haunts me to think of the power adults have over their lives when we are so lost ourselves.

What makes all of this injury so much worse is that it largely goes unseen (or unacknowledged). On Monday, April 24, 2023, Prime Minister Trudeau told a crowded room of University of Ottawa students that he never forced anyone to get vaccinated. In that moment, four years of moral injury was compounded. Not only did we suffer the moral harms of a society divided and the personal injury done to those who were vaccinated under coercion or even against their will (in the case of some children, elderly and mentally infirm), but now we must undergo the harm of one of the perpetrators denying that it ever happened, which creates a "double trauma." While we are still processing and grieving the harms of the last four years, now we must process and grieve their denial.

For some, that processing involves self-doubt. Did I just imagine what happened over the last four years? Was my job really at risk? Was travel really restricted? Are the shots really harming people or am I being unduly suspicious? Going forward, can I trust myself? Or should I trust authorities more?

This is what gaslighting does. It is wholly destabilizing, under-cutting our belief in our own abilities to see a situation for what it is. Gaslighters confuse their victims into submission or into questioning their own sanity, or both. Victims of the COVID-19 narrative are not only victims of state-sanctioned physical and psychological abuse; they are also victims of the denial that any of it ever happened.

MORAL REPAIR

At the end of her email to me, Beth elaborated on the residual feelings that linger for her after being closed out by her friend:

Many months after the failed plans with my friend and her daughter, I ran into them at a park. We had fallen out of contact but made pleasant conversation while the girls played. I felt guarded in a way that I have never experienced, but we were able to connect over common interests and small talk. During the course of our conversation, she disclosed that she had recently come back from a holiday by plane and gotten Covid. I remarked something about always getting sick on the plane, to which she replied, "No, we were already sick when we got on the plane." I knew then that that relationship could not be spared. That she would knowingly expose a plane load of people to the same illness for which she discriminated against my children was more cognitive dissonance than I could bear.

And the reality was that what she had done to my family and the things that had happened to us were completely invisible to her.

Invisible. Still in this moment, perhaps especially in this moment, so many feel invisible. When the world finally kept turning, there were colleagues who never returned, apologies that were never uttered, disinvites that were long forgotten. There were revisionist accounts that "it was only privileges" that were suspended and occasionally flat-out denial of the discriminations that transpired.

But most of all nothing. No acknowledgement, no amends, no promises that it would never happen again.

And for those still nursing deep wounds, a feeling of being completely invisible.

COVID reminded us that the repertoire of ways we are able to hurt each other is vast and varied, from the horrors of a child dead from vaccine injury to the petty ways we virtue-signal our disgust at fellow shoppers to severing playdates with unacceptable offspring. COVID turned us into seasoned destroyers of others' education, reputation, relationships and even self-worth.

Where can we possibly go from there? What salve is there for these injuries to our souls?

The process of moving from a situation where harm has occurred — the moral injury — to a situation where some degree of stability in moral relations is regained is typically called "moral repair." It's a process of restoring trust and hope in relationships and in oneself. If we have violated the normative expectations that keep us responsive and responsible to each other, then how can we repair the damage? How can we make amends?

On a personal level, I don't know if repair is possible with some of the relationships in my life. When my story broke in the Fall of 2021, far worse than losing my job or being shamed by the media was the shame that came from colleagues (e.g. "Shame on Julie Ponesse") and even friends. When a pattern of respect and discussion and genuine inquiry is dismissed in a moment with the label "grifter," or even "murderer," is repair possible? Should you even want it? And when such distrust settles in, is it possible ever to be open again? I often wonder, how have I let fear and shaming and apathy change me, and how will the new person I am face and endure challenges (and triumphs) in the future?

There are two important things to keep in mind as we search for ways to repair our injuries. One is that, as research shows, wrongdoers rarely apologize for moral harms; in fact, apology is the exception to regular patterns of human conduct, not the rule. So morally repairing ourselves is, as a matter of fact, unlikely to begin with an apology by those who have injured us.

The other is that some injuries are so deep they may simply be "beyond repair." Some victims of physical abuse can never hear a piece of music without thinking of their abuser. COVID may have revealed that the clash of values between partners makes their relationship unrepairable. And it has wiped from the face of the earth souls that will never walk it again. Their departure created breaks in family chains and social circles, voids where there ought to have been marriages and births and college graduations and big and little life projects and joys and sorrows. Some of the effects of our moral injuries are so deeply entrenched that they will simply be beyond repair.

HOPING FOR HOPE

On October 4, 1998, thousands in the Montreal area turned out for the unveiling of a monument called "Reparations," the first structure to the Armenian Genocide to be erected in a public place in Canada. While most post-genocidal emotions sit firmly on the negative side of the register — shame, terror, despair, rage, vengefulness, cynicism — the monument's creator, Arto Tchakmakdjian, said, somewhat surprisingly, that the meaning of the statue is hope.

There is a lot of talk these days of rebuilding trust and of the importance of hope as a way forward after what we've been through. And for good reason. If relationships are largely about the confidence we have that those we trust are trustworthy, then we need to remain optimistic that they are deserving of that trust, and that our world will allow our expectations about the future to be played out.

Walker, who has written extensively about repair in the aftermath of mass trauma, describes hope as "a desire that some perceived good come to realization; a belief that it is at least (even if barely) possible; and an alert openness to, absorption in, or an active pursuit of, the desired possibility."[53] Hope, she says, is essential for moral repair.

Hope is a fascinating and paradoxical emotion. First and foremost, it requires induction, the belief that the future will roughly resemble the past. From the late Old English *hopa*, hope is a kind of "confidence in the future." In order to hope, we need to believe that the future will in certain basic ways resemble the past; otherwise, it's too hard to make sense of things. But hope also requires an element of uncertainty; if we are certain about what will happen, then we expect it, we don't hope for it. Hope puts us in the precarious position of putting a great deal of emotional stock in something that is at least partly beyond our control.

But this raises for us a variety of crippling questions:

- How can you maintain hope and trust in a world that continues to disappoint?
- How can you have confidence in others to meet expectations when they have so frequently defected from them?
- How can you achieve unity with those you disagree with so profoundly?
- How do you move on in a world in which you can no longer take it for granted that our core institutions are fundamentally trustworthy?
- How can you try for moral repair when most deny that moral injury has occurred?
- How can you start to heal when you aren't sure the harm is over?

As much as I want to feel hope in this moment, I don't feel ready for it. Maybe I'm still too fragile. Maybe we all are.

Whenever the government releases a new statement, my reflex thought is "Hmm, probably not." And it doesn't feel good to be that distrusting. I don't want to throw the baby out with the bathwater and yet it feels safer to do so when the bathwater has proven itself so putrid.

Hope feels like too much for right now. It feels disingenuous, presumptuous, or even cruel, like it's interfering with a mourning process we should be left alone to have.

"SITTING IN THE L"

When you have been hurt, it is natural to want to start bandaging your wounds right away, to "buck up" and move forward. When asked "How are you?," how often do you say "okay" when the truth is that you are barely holding it together?

The scale of the COVID harms is so unfathomable that we find ourselves in an awkward middle ground between processing what has happened and figuring out what to do next. We are straddling the past and the future, mourning the loss of what could have been with the reality of what is now possible in the future. In the meantime, we are left with the messy feelings of loss seeping through the bandages we try in vain to wrap around our wounds. So, what can we do?

The 2nd century Roman emperor and Stoic Marcus Aurelius advised not to work too hard to distract ourselves from difficult feelings. The Stoics understood well that trying to cheat ourselves out of emotions like grief is a fool's errand. Buying a new Stanley water cup, doom-scrolling, taking a vacation, or remaining within the boundaries of 'proper' conversation will drive them away for a while but they won't fix what's really broken in us.

Instead of pushing ourselves to move on inauthentically, clinical psychologist Tara Brach suggests taking a "sacred pause" — suspending activity and tuning into our emotions — even in the midst of a fit of anger or sorrow. Psychotherapists and addiction recovery specialists call it "feeling the feelings" or "sitting in the L (loss)." Though our fast-paced world is largely intolerant of anything that causes us to slow and reflect, the idea is that, by suspending activity for a while, we can start to process what's happened to us and move forward with greater clarity.

TELLING OUR STORIES

Though it's a bit trite to say, two undeniable truths are that we can't control what others do and we can't change the past. We can wish things were different, we can imagine that others have better intentions than they do, but we can't ultimately control either. Sometimes we need to take up our own gauntlet and forge ahead in the absence of apology from those who harmed us. And sometimes we need to create hope for ourselves in a world that offers little reason for it.

The poet Maya Angelou, who lost the ability to speak for five years after being raped as a child, writes about how she cured herself of the cynicism it caused. Angelou says there is nothing quite so tragic as cynicism "because it means the person has gone from knowing nothing to believing nothing."[54] But Angelou says she didn't collapse under the weight of her cynicism. In those five years, she read and memorized every book she could get from the "white school library:" Shakespeare, Poe, Balzac, Kipling, Cullen and Dunbar. By reading the stories of others, she says she was able to create her own courage; she drew enough from the disappointments and triumphs of others to triumph herself.

Recovery by reading the stories of others? It's amazing how much moral power can exist in such a simple act.

I remember vividly Highwire host Del Bigtree reading aloud an eloquent letter to the unvaccinated: "If Covid were a battlefield, it would still be warm with the bodies of the unvaccinated."[55] True, I remember thinking, but lying there alongside them would be the bodies of anyone who dared to question, who refused to outsource their thinking, who kept trudging through the darkness without a lantern to light the way.

Moral endurance is a big problem these days. Those who have been speaking out are growing tired, and we don't even know what round of the fight we are in. Freedom fighters today are weary of endless Zoom calls and Substack articles rehearsing the mistakes of the last few years. Aren't we just overstuffing the echo chamber? Will any of it really matter? With the injury of time, even the most devout can fall away, and what once seemed to be the noblest of goals can start to lose vividness in the haze of unrelenting attacks and competition for our attention.

I find myself thinking a lot these days about how history will remember us, how it will remember the doctors who allowed themselves to be controlled by the state, the public servants who 'passed the buck,' and those of us who keep ringing the bell of freedom even when it doesn't resound. Will vindication ever come? Will balance ever be restored to the social order? Will the wounds of the last few years ever heal?

I don't have satisfying answers to any of these questions. And I'm sorry for that. But one thing I do know is that the war we are fighting won't be fought across the aisles of our parliaments, in our newspapers or in the boardrooms of Big Pharma. It will be fought between estranged sisters, between friends uninvited from Christmas gatherings, and between distanced spouses trying to see something vaguely familiar in the person sitting across from them at dinner. It will be fought as we struggle to protect our children and give our parents dignity in their last days. It will be fought in our souls. This is a war between the people, over whose lives matter, over what we are and can be, and over what sacrifices we expect each other to make.

Trish Wood, who moderated the Citizens' Hearing at which Kelly-Sue Oberle testified, wrote that a week later she still felt shaken by the magnitude of what she heard: the stories of silenced doctors who tried to advocate for their patients, the stories of men and women whose lives were forever changed by vaccine injury and, most tragically, the stories of those like Dan Hartman whose teenage son died following mRNA vaccination. Trish wrote about the importance of telling these stories, of taking account. "Bearing witness," she wrote, "is our power against the COVID cartel catastrophe."[56]

Trish's words are reminiscent of those of Auschwitz survivor Elie Wiesel. In the aftermath of the Holocaust, at a time when the world was so broken and so eager for a new beginning, Wiesel saw it as his responsibility to speak for those who had been silenced. He wrote, "I believe firmly and profoundly that whoever listens to a witness becomes a witness, so those who hear us, those who read us must continue to bear witness for us. Until now, they're doing it with us. At a certain point in time, they will do it for all of us."[57]

The lesson from Wood and Wiesel is that telling our stories is important, not just to set the record straight. It is a balm to our wounds. It's hard to know what to do with the residue of chaotic and intense emotions post-trauma. One thing that trauma and moral injury and tragic flaws all have in common is that naming them gives you power over them. You cannot heal what you cannot name. Once you name your trauma, you might find the courage to share your experiences with others, or it might be in the sharing of your experiences that you are able to name it. Adam, in the creation story, makes this point salient; he named the animals and then he had dominion over them.

The stories told at the Citizens' Hearing (2022), the Public Order Emergency Commission (2022), and the National Citizens Inquiry (2023) help not just to rebalance the public record; they also reify suffering into language. These stories — "trauma narratives," as Susan Brison calls them — help to create moral spaces for solidarity and connection and, ultimately, help to remake the self.[58] They convert the experience of injury and isolation into a community of speakers and listeners helping us to feel, at the very least, that we are not uniquely victimized. And there is moral repair even in that.

This is probably why the Freedom Convoy was so successful. People were finally able to share their stories with a group of like-minded people who weren't going to judge them for telling their stories out loud. That's powerful. It's like finally releasing toxins from your body, like a great purge of darkness.

"SOMEBODY, AFTER ALL, HAD TO MAKE A START"

On February 22, 1943, a 21 year-old German student named Sophie Scholl was convicted of high treason and condemned to death for distributing leaflets decrying Nazi crimes. She was executed by guillotine at 5 pm on the same day.

During her trial, Sophie was recorded as saying: "Somebody, after all, had to make a start. What we wrote and said is also believed by many others. They just don't dare express themselves as we did."

Sophie's words were a prelude to an era of repair that, in some sense, we are still living. I believe that the broken parts of us that made the atrocities of Nazi Germany both possible and deniable are still broken today.

History offers countless examples — leprosy stigma, Jim Crow laws, and the Holocaust, to name only a few — of a compliant and demoralized people slowly dehumanized by the obsession to distance ourselves from each other. Yet we can't seem to come to terms with the fact that we are living out yet again the moral weaknesses to which we have always been vulnerable.

Those who are doing the hard work of trying to bring attention to the unspeakable harms of the last four years might only be able to take the first few steps towards the repair we so badly need. And that repair will undoubtedly look different for each of us. For some, it will be a matter of fine-tuning a relatively efficient system. For others, it will look like retreat and recovery, and for others still it might require wholesale reinvention. Some will have to work to generate courage out of timidity, while others will need to reign in a frustrated and incendiary spirit.

And we shouldn't expect that any of this will happen quickly or easily. I think it will be a long time before the choir of humanity sings our praises, if it ever does.

It is all too easy, when in the middle of a crisis, to give up because it seems that we are failing, because it's hard to see the big picture from your small little vantage point. But to fix what ails us, we don't have to fix everything in one moment or one action... nor could we if we tried.

We only need to make a start.

Our Last Innocent Moment

All things truly wicked start from innocence.

—Ernest Hemingway, *A Moveable Feast*

It takes one second for a raindrop to fall 32 feet and 3-6 seconds to take a breath. My daughter was born into the world in a moment and the viral video that set my life on a new path was 4:53 minutes long. Our lives are made up of moments, some more meaningful, or at least more memorable, than others. Some slip into oblivion as soon as they happen while others punctuate our existence, reframing or redirecting our lives.

On March 11, 2020 everything changed. The eerie pandemic future that became our reality shifted our lives in what felt like a moment. Car consoles littered with dirty masks, downtowns deserted in the middle of the day. COVID-19 dropped us into a twilight zone of unquestionable science, the plaything of our era's spin doctors, and the realization of Sartre's theatric line: "Hell is other people."

In that moment, something light and innocent was lost. COVID-19 became a shared cultural flashpoint akin to 9/11, or the assassinations of John F. Kennedy or Martin Luther King, changing us almost instantaneously. We saw things about the world that we can never unsee. The dream of personal freedom died or, worse, maybe it had never been alive.

But unlike the bullet that kills only its victim, COVID slowly assassinated our way of life. In a moment we went from feeling stable to unsafe, oblivious to suspicious, and unable to escape the foreboding question, "What's next?" We underwent what ethicist Susan Brison calls a "radical undoing of the self," a disruption of what we remember and who we are, and a jarring separation of past from present. We became a tribe of barbarians seemingly overnight, but a tribe barely able to know who we are or to imagine that what we do means anything.

How did things shift so radically in one moment? Were we really that innocent before and, if so, what have we lost (and gained) in losing our innocence?

BLACK SWAN, WHITE SWAN

Though it may have felt like it, COVID didn't, all on its own, turn a previously liberal society into a cult of compliance; it merely exposed a war that has long been waging against personal liberty. As the pseudonymous blogger Sue Dunham wrote, "Since 9/11, every threat to come down the mainstream news cycle seemed to huddle us around the same consensus, that some fresh element of our liberty was making the world hurt—and that we were selfish to hold on to it." Time has been slowly evicting us from the idea that our personal rights, including our right to be, and be seen, as individuals, are inviolable.

If we want to understand how our innocence was shattered, then we need first to understand how we came to feel so safe and so trusting in the first place.

The downside to innocence is that it creates a certain opacity, shielding us from information that we might be better off to have. One reason 'fact-checking' became so popular, I think, is that it creates a normal distribution, or bell curve, of the information we receive from the world. It imposes some order on a messy world, allowing us to sweep away the complicated parts of life so we can move on less encumbered. Or, at least, it legitimizes ignoring the world's messiness. But this ignorance allows us to be caught off guard by events that we don't expect. And, when those events do occur, we interpret them as anomalies, disasters (if they are bad), or even black swan events (if they are extreme).

'Black swan' is a term coined by the statistician and risk analyst Nicholas Taleb[59] to describe a high-impact event that is deemed improbable and yet has massive consequences. Though 'black swans' feel unpredictable at the time, in retrospect they are often rationalized as having been avoidable. Black swans can be negative (e.g. 9/11 or Black Monday 1987), positive (the fall of the Berlin Wall) or neutral (e.g. the exponential growth of the internet).

COVID-19 has been called the black swan event of our time. *The Guardian's* Larry Elliott, for example, titled a January 2021 article "The 'black swan' Covid catastrophe shows us just how fragile our world is.' And reasonably so. COVID had an extreme impact on every sphere of life. It shut down governments and the economy, changed professional practice and, almost overnight, turned us into a draconian society of broken souls so dependent on government direction that we sacrificed ourselves and our loved ones for the sake of getting along and getting by.

But all is not quite as it seems. Taleb told Bloomberg Television in March 2020 that COVID was actually a 'white swan' if ever there was one. A 'black swan,' he reminded the interviewer, is a "rare, catastrophic event," not "a cliché for any bad thing that surprises us." Taleb coauthored a paper in January 2020 in which he claimed that several factors made the spread of COVID quite predictable: increased global connectivity, asymptomatic carriers, and a fatalistic public health response. For a risk analyst, that a pathogen should spiral out of control is hardly surprising.

Whether or not COVID was a true black swan event is not my focus here. Biology aside, I'm interested in Taleb's more general epistemological point that what catches us off guard would not have done so if we had a different perspective of the world.

I'm interested in what we knew (and didn't know) going into 2020, where our focus was and wasn't, and how this created the experience of being caught off guard.

WHAT SURPRISES THE TURKEY DOESN'T SURPRISE THE BUTCHER

One of the most interesting aspects of Taleb's book is that whether or not an event is considered to be a 'black swan' is almost wholly perceiver dependent. As Taleb quips, what may be a 'black swan' surprise for a turkey is not a 'black swan' surprise for its butcher. (Our goal should be to identify our blind spots in order to "avoid being the turkey.")[60]

Taleb writes that, although we tend to be quite good at turning information we receive into meaningful data, we also tend to be narrow-minded in our beliefs about the world, which makes us dogmatic and therefore prone to surprise. But there aren't as many surprises as we might think, not as many 'unknown unknowns' as 'known unknowns.'[61]

In other words, the possibility of a black swan event occurring pivots on epistemology, on what we know about the world at a given moment. Whether COVID is a black or white swan, whether and how it shattered our innocence, depends largely on what we knew, versus what we could have known (or *should* have known), going into 2020.

As I was sitting down to write this section, the email hit my inbox announcing that the recipients for this year's Nobel Prize in Physiology or Medicine are Katalin Kariko and Drew Weissman who developed the technology that led to the mRNA COVID vaccines.

The Nobel Prize is arguably the most scientifically prestigious award in the world and the honorees typically are, or become, legends in their fields, allowing other important discoveries to be built on them (e.g. Albert Einstein was awarded the prize in 1921 largely for his discovery of the photoelectric effect, which influenced the development of electron microscopes and solar cells).

How helpful it would be if we lived in a world in which the awarding of a Nobel Prize was an infallibly reliable indication of a discovery's safety and usefulness. Unfortunately, it isn't. Sometimes the pattern fails. In 1949, the brain surgeon Antonio Egas Moniz was awarded the Nobel Prize for his development of prefrontal leukotomy (i.e. lobotomy) in the treatment of schizophrenia, the efficacy and safety of which is now seriously doubted.[62] And the Nobel Prizes for peace awarded to Henry Kissinger and Yasser Arafat are now widely regarded as morally dubious. That said, the Nobel foundation does not rescind prizes. So Kariko and Weissman will forever have their prize regardless of what the future shows about the safety and usefulness of their discovery.

What's my point? It is partly that awarding the Nobel Prize to those who discovered the technology that made the mRNA vaccines possible is a reflection of what we think we know now about the technology, not what is true absolutely. Time might tell us whether our confidence is well placed. Or it might not. Either way, it is easy to forget that even Nobel Prizes are the result of an unavoidably imperfect process: they are typically awarded quickly after the discovery, leaving little time to evaluate its long-term implications, and they are the result of human choice.

How will history look on the 2023 prize, I wonder? Will our confidence turn out to be well-placed or will we find that we are the turkey with a black swan surprise?

IN PLAIN SIGHT

One of the things we have learned over the last four years is just how much regulatory capture factored into the COVID response, how economics turned vaccine technology into an industrial profit machine. One crucial piece of evidence for this came from the Pfizer report, released last year by the FDA as part of a U.S. court order,[63] containing what Naomi Wolf calls "evidence of the greatest crime against humanity in the history of our species."

The report shows massive incongruity between how the

vaccines were marketed to the public and what Pfizer knew about them prior to their release to market. It shows:

- Pfizer knew their gene-based injections had negative efficacy as early as November 2020 (with the third most common side effect of the vaccine being COVID, itself)
- shortly after the vaccines came to market, Pfizer hired 2,400 full-time employees to process the adverse event reports (a stunning fact given the culture of silence that prevented so many adverse events even from being reported to, or processed by, physicians)
- that the vaccines cause myocarditis within a week after injection
- the shot's lipid nanoparticles do not remain at the injection site but are quickly biodistributed throughout the body to the brain, liver, spleen, and ovaries where they may remain permanently
- an asymmetry between the adverse events that were disclosed to the public (chills, fatigue, swelling at injection site) and those contained in the documents (haemorrhages, blood clots, neurological disorders, Bell's Palsy, Guillain-Barré syndrome)
- there were 61 deaths from stroke, half of which took place within 48 hours of injection

These are the things Pfizer knew. These are the things Pfizer did not reveal to the public. These are the things that made us the turkeys and Pfizer, the butcher.

It has been said that there is no historical parallel to the COVID vaccines: a vigorously marketed experimental product on a global scale, which garnered almost perfect support from policymakers. The scale of money involved is almost beyond comprehension. Pfizer's 2023 "Annual Review" states: "2022 was a year in which we set all-time highs in several financial categories." That year, Pfizer's revenue was a record-setting $100.3 billion, 38% coming from the Pfizer-BioNTech vaccine.

While it's no secret that pharmaceutical companies spend large portions of their budgets on marketing, it's hard to think of pharmaceutical products being marketed like cars or lipstick. But they are. Perhaps even more so. In 2022, Pfizer spent $2.8 billion on marketing, a mere 2% of the revenue they earned from the Pfizer-BioNTech vaccine. But just how pharmaceutical products are marketed is a complex business.

One thing we find in the Pfizer report is a long list of donations to organizations that encouraged vaccine use, and/or directly addressed vaccine hesitancy. Pfizer couldn't produce ads endorsing mandates — that would have been too obvious — but they could fund various lobbying groups, healthcare colleges, media, and even medical journals that promote vaccine use, address vaccine hesitancy, and support mandates.

Among Pfizer's charitable donations, the report lists: $200,000 to the American Academy of Paediatrics, $100,000 to the American College of Emergency Physicians for Vaccine confidence PSAs, and $337,550 to the American Lung Association's Pneumonia Awareness Campaign. (If you want to promote the uptake of a vaccine for a respiratory virus, it makes strategic sense to advertise pneumonia as a severe side effect of COVID.)

It is also noteworthy that Pfizer is a regular contributor to universities, most of which mandated their product. When the newspapers started to report my story in the fall of 2021, the Toronto Star contacted Arthur Caplan, Director of Medical Ethics at NYU Medical Centre, for a comment. His response was "I've been working on vaccines for 9 years and I wouldn't pass her in my class." What I have since discovered is that Pfizer donated $20,000 to NYU for a program to counter misinformation about COVID-19 vaccine. Caplan's salary is, therefore, paid by a university that received money directly from Pfizer to promote the uptake of its COVID vaccine.

We have a similar situation in Canada. In 2020, Pfizer Canada made a $600K donation to the McGill "Interdisciplinary Initiative in Infection and Immunity" (M14). M14 promotes COVID vaccine uptake and Pfizer funds M14. And "19toZero," an "independent, non-profit organization" aimed at increasing vaccine confidence, states on their website (albeit in very fine print): "…This portal has been funded by a pharmaceutical grant provided by Moderna Canada."

Back to the issue of perspective. What we knew, and didn't know, during the COVID crisis about the severity of the virus, and the safety and efficacy of the technology developed to address it, was heavily influenced by the companies that stood to make the greatest financial gains from how we responded. Everything from how many companies enforced vaccine mandates to whether mothers would allow their children to play with unvaccinated friends impacted the bottom lines of companies like Pfizer and Moderna, and they seem to have acted accordingly and strategically.

But the fact that the pharmaceutical industry has been shaping health care policy through outside advocacy organizations is not a new phenomenon. Let me offer two examples of this phenomenon that existed in plain sight prior to 2020.

Example 1: The Opioid epidemic: Conservatively, opioids caused the deaths of half a million Americans in the last 20 years. Purdue Pharma, the maker of Oxycontin, aggressively promoted its use for decades despite clear evidence of its potential for addiction and overdose. Court documents revealed that Purdue spent over $200 million on advertising and sponsored 20,000 pain "education programs" in an effort to sway physicians to prescribe more opioids. Five years after its release, OxyContin had generated an annual revenue of more than $1 billion.

Example 2: Tamiflu: During the 2005 avian flu outbreak, Evan Morris, a former lobbyist for Genentech (the company that sells Tamiflu for Roche), reportedly[64] paid third-party groups to generate fears about the virus and the need for the government to stockpile Tamiflu. Dozens of U.S. Senators wrote to President George W. Bush about their concerns, and the president authorized an emergency stockpile that bought $1 billion of the antiviral medication.

These occurrences of collusion between the medical profession and the pharmaceutical industry might seem surprising but the information was hardly lurking in the shadows. In 2002, editor-in-chief of the *New England Journal of Medicine* Arnold Seymour Relman wrote:

"The medical profession is being bought by the pharmaceutical industry, not only in terms of the practice of medicine but also in terms of teaching and research. The academic institutions of this country are allowing themselves to be the paid agents of the pharmaceutical industry."

And four years before that, Dr. Matthias Rath wrote in the *Journal of the American Medical Association*:

"Throughout the 20th century, the pharmaceutical industry has been constructed by investors, the goal being to replace (and outlaw) effective but non-patentable natural remedies with mostly ineffective but patentable and highly profitable pharmaceutical drugs. The very nature of the pharmaceutical industry is to make money from ongoing diseases."

In more quantitative terms, the *British Medical Journal* in 2017 showed that 50% of editors of the world's most influential medical journals were receiving money from the pharmaceutical industry.[65]

What all of this should have taught us going into 2020 is that, just because something is on the market, doesn't mean it is safe. Just because a product is vigorously marketed or highly profitable, doesn't mean it is safe. And just because a product is endorsed by a university or medical college, or even by the Nobel committee, doesn't mean it is safe. On the contrary, the evidence shows that collusion between drug companies and major institutions was common long before 2020. The fact that both the severity of COVID as a virus, and the safety and effectiveness of the COVID shots were vastly overestimated should never have surprised us. They were the white swans of 21st century medicine. And they shouldn't have shattered our innocence because it is information we should have had a clear hold on in the first place.

WHY SO NAIVE?

One lesson black swan events teach is just how fragile are our systems of thought. Being innocent of the contents of the Pfizer report and of the history of pharmaceutical collusion, more generally, makes the harms of the COVID response not just extreme but tragic, because they were foreseeable and, therefore, preventable. The truth is that, whether we saw, or didn't see, relevant information is what helped to create the COVID harms. We were complicit. And there are two common, and quite reasonable, ways of thinking that made us prone to being caught off guard in the ways that we were.

One is the idea that the past is a reliable predictor of the future. One of the most powerful pieces of propaganda in the COVID response was "All vaccines on the market are safe, therefore the COVID vaccine is safe too." We are vulnerable to this error in thinking because of our belief that the future will roughly resemble the past. And for many things in life, this is a reasonable way of forming beliefs. But it isn't an infallible one. As the philosopher Bertrand Russell pointed out in 1948, with respect to certain phenomena — markets and stock prices, for example — a pattern in the past is no guarantee of that pattern holding true in the future. The observance of a single black swan negated the long-held presumption that all swans we will see will be white. A set of conclusions can easily be undone once any of its fundamental premises is proven false. Our belief that something being on the market, or being endorsed by an institution (or even the totality of institutions), makes it safe, unfortunately is not a reliable indication that it is so.

The second common way of thinking that allowed us to be caught off guard is that we are vulnerable to "salience bias," which predisposes us to misjudging the importance or likelihood of events by giving excessive weight to information that is more obvious. Commercial air travel is statistically 1,000 times safer than driving a car. But most people are more afraid of flying as plane crashes are, in some sense at least, more dramatic and more salient. The problem with salience bias is that it distorts our perception, memory, problem-solving abilities, and ultimately, our decision-making.

When it came to COVID decision-making, salience bias came into play as we began to give disproportionate attention to information about infections and deaths, which were widely publicized, versus information about vaccine side effects and the negative impacts of COVID restrictions, which were not. Our collective disregard for the less salient information became so perilous that, in May 2020, a group of over 600 physicians sent a letter[66] to President Trump pointing out that "the downstream health effects…are being massively underestimated and under-reported." The authors called the lockdowns a "mass casualty incident" with "exponentially growing negative health consequences." The negative effects of the COVID response, the authors claimed, were being massively under-estimated and under-reported.

In reality, suicide hotline calls and liquor sales both increased by 600% and 150,000 Americans per month experienced missed cancer diagnoses. "This is an order of magnitude error," the authors wrote. The letter was signed by over 500 physicians including Richard Amerling, Marilyn Singleton, and Amit Gupta. But this letter, like all other attempts to point out the harmful consequences of the response, went largely ignored.

NUDGE, NUDGE,…

In a perfect world, or at least a world more perfect than our own, choices about our health and how to treat others during COVID would have been made by weighing available evidence in light of our deeply held beliefs and values. In the real world, something quite different happened.

In 2010, a decade before most of us ever heard of "COVID," members of what is now called the "Behavioural Insights Team" in the UK were commissioned by the Cabinet Office, along with academics from the London School of Economics, to author a report on how to influence behaviour. The result was "MIND-SPACE,"[67] a report which explores how policymakers can harness nine of the most powerful ways of influencing behaviour. I think you might find it interesting to see the full list:

1. **Messenger**: we are heavily influenced by who is communicating information (e.g. using celebrities, 'experts,' and other trusted members of the community in vaccine confidence campaigns)

2. **Incentives**: Our response to incentives is shaped by predictable mental shortcuts, such as the strong desire to avoid losses (e.g. the social currency of wearing a mask)

3. **Norms**: We often align our actions with what we perceive as 'normal' within our social group (e.g. seeing and sharing vaccine 'stickers' on social media)

4. **Defaults**: We tend to take the path of least resistance (e.g. it was much easier to "go with the flow," to follow the narrative, than it was to resist it)

5. **Salience**: We tend to pay more attention to what is novel, relevant, or conspicuous (e.g. we were told to focus on COVID severity and harms, and on distancing, masking and vaccination, so we did)

6. **Priming**: Our actions can be subtly influenced by subconscious cues in our environment (e.g. images of giddy-looking people

getting vaccinated helped to prime our COVID attitudes about the safety, and immunological and social value, of vaccination)

7. **Affect**: Our actions can be powerfully shaped by our emotions (e.g. distancing so as to avoid killing the grandmother we love dearly)

8. **Commitments**: We like to act in ways that align with our commitments (e.g. following the narrative was the way to be 'in it' with others, to 'do our part')

9. **Ego**: We tend to act in ways that make us feel better about ourselves (e.g. masking, distancing and vaccinating supports a desire to be, and to be seen as, useful, helpful, and even a saviour)

Well beyond 'carrots and sticks,' nudging became the new way to implement policy changes by influencing our behaviour. To this day, the Behavioural Insight Team admits that the MINDSPACE report "continues to be used by the Behaviour Insights as a framework to aid the application of behavioural science to the policymaking process."[68]

Looking back over the last four years, it's not hard to see how these nudges worked together to create a powerful propaganda machine. If you combine the omnipresent talk of the imminent danger of a global pandemic with the fact that we are naturally prone to confirmation bias[69]— we tend to search for evidence that confirms the beliefs we already have — you have a powerful influencer of behaviour. If you are pro-narrative, you were likely to see the current spike in myocarditis and all-cause mortality as long-term effects of long-COVID; if you are anti-narrative, you were more likely to interpret these as vaccine injuries.

In general, our lives are shaped by an inescapable confluence of narrative, bias, and choice. The choices we make have hefty effects on our actions and, to a certain extent, our character, but those choices are powerfully shaped by the biases we have about the world and the stories we tell ourselves to make sense of it. We process all of this information through elaborate mental acrobatics, making decisions about what's best based on an incomplete picture of the relevant factors, black holes of evidence we need to fill in order to form more accurate beliefs about the world.

Finding a black swan would not be surprising were it not for the belief that all swans are white. The COVID response would not have caught us off guard were it not for the beliefs that institutions are infallibly good and our choices are always our own.

BILDUNGSROMAN

"Innocence" is a loaded word. In law, it refers to a lack of guilt. But, for me, that's its least interesting sense. In art and literature, innocence is often contrasted with a lack of experience, as in the case of children who are not yet wise to the harms and villains of the world. (Think of Bouguereau's *L'Innocence* painting or the philosopher Rousseau's description of "childhood as a time of innocence.")

L'Innocence. 1893. William Adolphe Bouguereau

But innocence can also refer to an optimistic way of looking at the world. Ignorance is bliss, they say. Or as the 1st century BC Latin writer Publilius Syrus said "In knowing nothing, life is most delightful."

In literature, innocence is often portrayed as a thing lost in a larger coming of age story — a "Bildungsroman." It is a vehicle for working out what troubles us, even if what troubles us are the harms caused by our own innocence. Characteristic of these coming of age stories is a rite of passage to set the stage for an epiphany, or awakening.

The *Iliad* is a Bildungsroman, some say the first. It isn't just the story of the Trojan War. The war is a backdrop for the story of Achilles' development. At the beginning, Achilles is a foolhardy youth, making costly decisions for himself and those around him. He loses his best friend Patroclus in battle and then spends much of the story inwardly torturing himself because of it. The story ends when he reaches maturity and allows Priam to recover Hector's body.

Ian McEwan's *Atonement* similarly depicts a loss of innocence over time. The novel's protagonist, Briony Tallis, misinterprets the adult interactions between her sister, Cecilia, and Robbie and, as a consequence, falsely accuses Robbie of controlling and coercing Cecilia and, later, of raping her cousin, Lola. Her inability to understand basic events in the world around her, augmented by her childish worldview, initiates a loss of innocence that she is never able to retrieve. Briony is changed by what she witnesses (or thinks she witnesses), by how she behaved as a result of it, and by the gradual realization of the destruction she has caused. As she grows and begins to understand what she has done, she suffers not just a loss of innocence but a loss of her own identity, and she spends the rest of her life attempting to atone for the mistakes she made as an innocent child.

In every loss of innocence story, there is a moment where the character starts to awaken to a new reality, which is usually somehow uncomfortable at first. Plato talks about the pain of emerging from the metaphorical 'cave' in which the things we believe to be real are really just shadows on a wall. The light of truth hurts our eyes so much that some opt to stay in the dark where things are, though false, more comfortable.

The last few years, for many, have been a process of awakening, like the first moments of waking up after a bad dream, where it hurts to look directly at the light. Maybe our innocence was due to a barrage of information that we couldn't process quickly enough, maybe to our scientism and perfectionism, or to a deadly combination of these. Whatever the cause, people will react to this awakening differently. Some will run towards the light, craving what they were missing all along. Others will resist it, trying everything possible to retreat to the simpler world. For many, cognitive dissonance might seem like the only method of self-preservation. It is human nature to make ourselves oblivious to inconvenient information. As Friedrich Nietzsche said of "motivated forgetting," man must forget in order to move forward.

Maybe this is what we are doing now. Maybe this is the motivation behind Emily Oster's call for COVID amnesty: "Let's focus on the future, and fix the problems we still need to solve." If you are starting to realize the hand you had in some harm, doesn't it make sense to call for a moratorium on blame? It might make sense but, if our focus on the future is making us blind to our complicity in the harms of the past, then we have a problem. Ultimately, we need to make a choice between two ways of living: willful but destructive ignorance versus enlightenment and meaning. And neither of these paths is without its troubles.

REFINEMENT BY FIRE

In a moment, COVID shattered our view of what the world is and how safe we can feel in it. The biggest obstacle to abandoning the narrative now is not that it is so undeniably compelling but because doing so would shatter a story that has immense apparent coherence: the world gathered around a viral crisis, imposed draconian measures for a noble reason, and mandated a panacean vaccine without which we might have been wiped out. If you remove even just one of these elements, the story falls apart. What if you took a vaccine with severe side effects to prevent a virus which, for most, is quite mild? What if the cure was worse than the disease? What if exposing yourself to the virus would have been a better choice than excommunicating your friends?

Over the last four years, we all told ourselves different stories. Stories are what give our lives meaning. They help us to make sense of a chaotic world. In a world gradually stripping itself of meaning, the COVID narrative gives us a common enemy, a reason to bind together, and to be each other's heroes and saviours. If we lose this story, we risk losing how we see ourselves and, worse still, how we give meaning to our lives. Believing the wrong story, or believing in a story that ultimately falls apart, puts not only our identity but our morality on the line.

To put this into some perspective, consider the following analogy to the process of chemical refinement. In order to become useful, metals such as iron, copper, and lead require oxidation. This is a process in which oxygen is added to impure liquid metal which then binds to the impurities so they can be removed. Just as oxygen is to liquid metal, so is truth to our perception of the world. When we start to allow truth to gain access to our contaminated perceptions, we begin the process of refinement and the falsities begin to fall away. This process is tumultuous, identity-altering and maybe even painful but the result, if we choose to undergo it, is a kind of purification.

As awful as it all was, one of the gifts COVID gave us is that it passed our view of the world and people in it through a filter. It refined through fire our relationships, our images of ourselves, and the trust we have in our core institutions and in each other. Personally, I became more independent and aware of needing to develop more self-sufficiency, but also more willing to invest in the relationships that have proven themselves. On the negative side, I have grown immensely less trusting of institutions and of my fellow citizens, and in some sense less able to muster the moral effort to make things work with people. Cynicism is a tough disposition to shake.

Now that we are beginning to see the world for what it is, we will never be able to approach it with the innocence we had. We have been forever changed. Innocence is for a particular stage of life. It is for children who have yet to grow up, to feel the burden of responsibility. We can mourn that loss. But we can't revel in it forever. Awakening to what's been happening is to awaken to who we are and who we have become in all its buzzing, frenetic confusion.

COVID shattered our innocence. That is true. But it also gave us a gift, an opportunity to choose the easy path of compliance or the enlightened path of growth and maturation. As William Blake says of innocence and experience, they are "the two contrary states of the human soul." You can't have both.

Which will you choose?

Babel Moments

*Come, let us build ourselves a city, with a tower that
reaches to the heavens, so that we may make a name for
ourselves; otherwise we will be scattered over the face of
the whole earth.*

—Genesis 11:4

*Oh we may have sharper tools
But we don't always know how to use them
After all we're only human*

—Matthew Barber, "Viral"

About 5,000 years ago, somewhere in the middle of the desert in the land of Shinar (south of what is now Baghdad, Iraq), a group of migrants decided to stop and build a city. One among them, quite possibly Nimrod,[70] suggested that they build a tower so tall it will reach to the heavens." But the Lord came down and, so displeased with what they were up to, confused their language and scattered them over the face of the earth.

In 2020, our modern civilization experienced a similar system failure on a global scale. We were building something. Or so it seemed. And then it all went terribly wrong. Now, bodies are invaded by the state, children are killing themselves, and the world is burning. We are more disconnected than ever before and we have lost our ability to communicate with each other. And yet our destruction is well masked in the pretence of progress and unity.

We seem to be having another "Babel Moment," a punctuated moment in history when excessive pride in our own abilities leads to our own destruction. Like other similar moments in history — the fall in Eden, the Late Bronze Age collapse, the Destruction of the Roman Empire — it's a story of the natural consequences of human ingenuity running ahead of wisdom. It's a story about misguided unification projects. It's a story echoed in so many of the fractures we see today: between the left and right, liberals and conservatives, Israelis and Palestinians, truth and lies. It's a story about what's breaking between us and within each of us.

I don't think it would be an overstatement to say that we are reeling. Like different tribes who inhabit the same country and are subject to the same laws, we have wildly different views about what it is to be good, whether we are citizens or subjects, whether history can teach us anything, and whether human life, in all its forms and at all of its stages, is sacred. We look at our neighbour and are disoriented, unable to understand the person staring back at us. We are a people adrift in a historical no-man's place, "unmoored" as Brett Weinstein poetically but hauntingly said. We are orphans of history, of liberty, and even of our own sense of conscience.

"...PILING MOUNTAINS UP TO THE DISTANT STARS"

The story of Babel, like so many in the Bible, is frustratingly brief, offering only a few lines and few specific clues about what the tower looked like, whether the Babylonians thought they succeeded or failed, and why their punishment was to be radically dispersed. Artists' renderings of the tower mimic the sort of prestige architecture that was common in the ancient world, possibly modelled on Etemenanki, a stone ziggurat the height of New York's Flatiron building dedicated to the Mesopotamian god Marduk. What we do know is how the story ended: God was so displeased that he confused their language and spread them as far apart from one another as they could be.

From Athanasius Kircher. Turris Babel... Amsterdam, 1679

Cautionary tales about the costs of human pride running amok are not unique to the Christian tradition. There is the love origins story from Plato's *Symposium* that I mentioned earlier, in which humans became "so lofty in their notions" that Zeus cut them in two leaving each one cursed to roam the earth searching for their other half.

Gigantomachy. Engraving by Virgil Solis for Ovid's Metamorphoses Book I, 151-161. Fol. 4r, image 6. PD-art-10

In Greek mythology, the "Gigantomachy" myth describes the desperate struggle between the Gigantes (giants) and the Olympian gods to rule over the universe. In Ovid's telling of the story, the twin giants Ephialtes and Otis attempt to reach the heavens by stacking the Ossa, Pelion, and Thessaly mountain ranges on top of one another. Ovid writes, "Rendering the heights of heaven no safer than the earth, they say the giants attempted to take the Celestial kingdom, piling mountains up to the distant stars."[71] But, clearly outmatching them, Jupiter shot his lightning bolts at them, hurling the mountains back to earth and drenching it with "streams of blood."

It isn't surprising that we keep telling and retelling the Babel story. It's a perennial human story, a cautionary tale of what happens when we get intellectually too 'big for our britches.' With all its skill and prowess to move us forward, the human intellect has one great flaw — it tends to worship what it produces, relying on its products to make us perfect, complete, and wholly self-sufficient. Why do so many biblical stories repeatedly warn against the practice of idolatry and, more importantly, why do we continue to make the same errors?

Today, the quantum leaps in technology on almost every front are dizzying. It seems that we are always taking the Babel steps "two at a time." In 1903, Orville Wright made a 12-second flight 20 feet above a wind-swept beach in North Carolina. A mere 96 years later, the Space Shuttle Discovery took a 3.2 million-mile voyage 340 miles above the earth. In the last century, advances in medicine and agriculture increased life expectancy in the U.S. by approximately 30 years, and more than doubled it in some jurisdictions. Technological wonders exploded everywhere.

And so did the horrors. In 1900, long-range artillery could fairly accurately hit targets only a few miles away. By the end of the century, we could launch long-range precision strikes with nuclear-capable missiles. And then, of course, drones allowed us to do this from an easy chair on the other side of the world. Aptly called the "Beastly Century," never in history were so many killed in such a short period of time.

Now, these technologies have taken exponential leaps. We can draw knowledge out of the internet at the touch of a few keys and communicate with anyone at a moment's notice. We can reach farther depths of the universe and the oceans, penetrate sub-cellular levels of the human body, grow meat in labs, print 3D organs, and conduct surgery by robots from just about anywhere in the world. And, as you read this, physicists in a suburb of Geneva (at CERN, The European Organization for Nuclear Research) are trying to collide particles at a rate fast enough to open a gateway to another dimension.

Then there is the exponential growth of Artificial Intelligence. When I last taught at university, using AI to write essays wasn't yet a reality. I can't imagine what it would be like now, trying to tease out a student's own work from AI-generated material. But consider where we could be in a few short decades. Most of the AI we use now is "weak AI," AI that can outperform human behaviour but only within a limited set of parameters and constraints (e.g. iPhone's Siri or Google's RankBrain). But some experts are euphorically predicting that, within our lifetime, Artificial Superintelligence, AI that can perform *any* task better than a human, will become the norm and could be used to eradicate disease and food shortages, colonize other planets, and make us bionic... and perhaps even immortal.

But that's a topic for another discussion. What I'm interested in here is how our near myopic focus on technology is connected to what happened on the plains of Shinar 5,000 years ago.

TOO BIG TO FAIL

When you read God's response at the climax of the Babel story, it might seem like a bit of an overreaction. He spread the Babylonians across the whole earth just for building a tower in the desert? Was it really that wrong to use their ingenuity in this way? Did God feel threatened by the tower, itself, or by their resourcefulness?

That's not likely if you believe the God of Genesis is omnipotent and, therefore, incapable of insecurity or jealousy. What's more likely is that Babel is a cautionary tale about the consequences of idolizing our intellect. It wasn't the tower, itself, that was a problem. We learn in the previous chapter in Genesis that Nimrod "began to be mighty in the earth" (10:8-9). The Babylonians wanted to make a tower as tall as humanly possible, or more accurately, *in*humanly possible. They built the tower to see what they could do, maybe even to make a name for themselves. Like the Greek Gigantes trying to reach the heavens, the problem was thinking they could interface with the heavens by their powers alone. "[N]othing that they propose to do will now be impossible for them" (11:6) foreshadows innovations far grander than a brick tower.

Thousands of years later, this arrogance culminated in the invincibility mantra "too big to fail," a term made popular by U.S. Congressman Steward McKinney in 1984. McKinney worried that the failure of our largest institutions would be so disastrous to the greater economic system that they should be supported by government when they face failure. The idea was not that these corporations are so big they cannot, as a matter of fact, fail but that our reliance on them means that we *ought* to do what we can to prevent their failure. Of course, Alan Greenspan famously objected, "If they're too big to fail, they're too big." But the idea had already taken hold.

Babel wasn't just a tower but an idea. And it wasn't just an idea of expansion and improvement; it was an idea of perfection and transcendence. It was an idea so lofty that it had to fail because it was no longer human. The Babylonians thought they could dissolve the distinction between heaven and earth, mortal and immortal, the transcendent and the mundane.

When it came to diagnosing the problem with the COVID shots, it's interesting that Heather Heying locates the problem not so much in our attempt to control a virus; the problem, she says, is that we had the audacity to think that our attempts to do so would be infallible. In a lovely email correspondence we had in November 2023, Heather graciously elaborated on her original idea. She wrote:

> Humans have been trying to control nature since we have been human; in many cases we have even met with moderate success. But our arrogance always seems to get in the way. The Covid shots were one such attempt. The attempt to control SARS-CoV2 may well have been an honest one, but the inventors of the shots ran into serious problems when they imagined themselves infallible. The solution was deeply flawed, and the rest of us weren't allowed to notice.

The problem with the shots, in Heying's mind, is the nature of the idea. And it is an idea that allowed for no caution, no questioning, and certainly no dissension.

Like the COVID shots that were made possible by the development of a new technology, it's interesting to me that it was also a significant technical advancement that allowed the Babylonians even to consider building their tower. The Babylonians had figured out how to make kiln-fired bricks whereas, in nearby Palestine, only sun-dried bricks had been used, typically with stone for the foundations[72]: "Come, let us make bricks, and burn them thoroughly."[73]

Whether on the plains of Shirah or in a lab in Marburg,[74] every so often faith in human technology outpaces our ability to focus and mold it. The "We can, so we will" attitude barrels us ahead without the guidance of whether "We should." And amidst it all, existentially and subconsciously, we toy with the idea of doing without something outside of, or greater than, ourselves. (I'll return to the idea of transcendence a little later.)

TOGETHER, APART

I have often wondered what it would have been like in Babel in the early days after its destruction. We don't know that God actually destroyed the tower but imagination conjures images of people wandering in the dust of the ruins, living in the rubble of failed hopes and broken dreams. "What now?" they must have wondered.

One interesting thing about the Babel story is that the tower was built not just as an hubristic attempt to reach heaven but to preserve unity among themselves. "Come, let us build ourselves a city and a tower…; otherwise we shall be scattered…" It's hard to blame them for that.

The COVID narrative revealed our own goal of unity, an ostensibly noble one: "We are all in this together," "Do your part." Though punctuated in 2020, a sociocultural shift towards a particular species of unity — unity by uniformity — started gaining momentum years before.

To accomplish a utopian human project as grand as Babel, creating a rip in time or eradicating a virus, there is little room for individual difference. If someone wants to take time to develop a different kind of brick or pause to consider the broader meaning of genetic manipulation, the momentum for the project would wane. Individualism — a sense of who one is apart from the group — is a threat to collective utopian projects and, since these are what define us now, it is the greatest threat to the ethos of our time. We are told that our individual lives are a reasonable sacrifice to make for the sake of a grand human project, and it's a sacrifice most people seem to be quite happy to make.

Why?

Because the trade-off is the promise of immortality, the promise of something greater than itself.

We are born, we make what we can out of our own little lives, we grow old, and then we die. Our time on earth passes in the blink of an eye and, unless you are a spiritual person, you believe that, when you die, that's it. So we try to prolong life artificially or we invest our identity in the stock of the group so that at least we may live on through others. "War is peace," "Freedom is slavery," "We are all in this together." Recite them enough and eventually they become the normal, even virtuous, way to inject meaning into our lives.

If we take a bird's eye view of human history, we can see a series of cycles between accelerations in reason and technology, and then decelerations and eventual decline. We innovate, we progress, and then we stagnate, and sometimes regress or even collapse. We developed tools, perfected metalworking, invented the printing press, and then the internet. Never has our world felt so large, yet also so interconnected and unified in language, lifestyle, and thought. In many ways, we are closer than ever to being "one people." But never, in my lifetime anyway, have things felt so precarious, and so aimless and futile. As Canadian songwriter Matthew Barber wrote recently: "Oh we may have sharper tools, But we don't always know how to use them, After all we're only human…"[75]

Babel isn't just a story about tribalism. It's a story about the loss of stability, about displacement to a new reality. It's a metaphor for what's happening not just between the right and the left, pro- and anti-narrative, but for what's shifting in our institutions, in our culture, and in ourselves. It's a story of alienation and brokenness.

Metaphorically, I don't know if we are living the days leading up to the tower's destruction or the days just after. But it's pretty clear that our disagreements with each other are core; when it comes to meaning and morality, we don't speak the same language on a very fundamental level.

I can't help but wonder, if humanity cycles through these Babel moments periodically, why? What do all these "Babel moments" have in common? Are we doomed to repeat them? And if we recognize the moment while we are in it, can we do something to change our course, to make the outcome less disastrous than it might otherwise be?

LOSING THE PLOT...

Personally, what I worry about most these days is not that we will experience some punctuated calamity — sudden economic collapse or nuclear war. Believe it or not, those are not our worst-case scenarios.

What I worry about most is that we've lost the plot, that we've forgotten how to live, and with all our focus on the ability of science to save us, we've lost the 'why' to our 'how.' I worry that our materialism, our progressivism, and our obsessive perfection-ism are incurring a debt we may not be able to pay. I worry that we will, one day, become victims of our own ingenuity.

A few months ago, I had the pleasure of reviewing Michael Bonner's *In Defence of Civilization,* a book about whether or not our civilization is on the verge of collapse. A gem of Bonner's book is his analysis of what goes wrong in the decades leading up to collapse. Bonner reminds us that civilizations are complex systems—of technology, economics, foreign relations, immunology, and civility—and the more complicated and efficient a system becomes, the more likely it is to collapse. The kingdoms of Mycenae in Greece, the Hittite empire in Anatolia, the Egyptian New Kingdom — even the most triumphant civilizations proved to be vulnerable to total destruction. And, more often than not, the destruction comes from internal factors, not outside invasions. As Edward Gibbons points out, the Roman Empire ultimately succumbed to barbarian invasions, but it was the gradual loss of civic virtue among its citizens that made it vulnerable.

Let's take a leap from Rome to Oceania, the fictional land of Orwell. One of the great lessons from *1984* is that the Inner Party doesn't kill its enemy. It doesn't need to. It does something far worse. It transforms him from the inside, stripping him of everything that made him fight, stand up, and want to live. As O'Brien, a member of the Party, says to Winston, the protagonist:

'You are a flaw in the pattern, Winston. You are a stain that must be wiped out. Did I not tell you just now that we are different from the persecutors of the past? We convert him, we capture his inner mind, we reshape him... By the time we had finished with them they were only the shells of men. There was nothing left in them except sorrow for what they had done, and love of Big Brother. It was touching to see how they loved him. They begged to be shot quickly, so that they could die while their minds were still clean.'[76]

One of the Party's most efficient strategies to keep people 'in line' is to instil the fear of personal annihilation. People disappear. They don't get a public execution, which would at least provide some historical record of their existence. They are simply extinguished. No one wants to become the disappeared, the unknown, the non-existed.

One of the things that keeps people in line today is living in a perpetual crisis mode. And, when in a crisis, it's hard to think for oneself and to focus on the things that give life meaning. As Abraham Maslow's "hierarchy of needs" shows, the higher needs (love and belonging, esteem, and self-actualization) start to emerge only once we have satisfied our more basic needs (safety and basic physiological needs). If we are worried about housing or the price of food or our physical safety, it will be hard to think about working on our relationships or developing personal projects.

Research is showing how COVID social distancing measures, in particular, sucked us into the bottom layers of the Maslow's pyramid, triggering a shift towards negative emotions. When asked which emotions they felt most during the early months of 2020, participants in a recent study[77] said that the emotions they felt with highest intensity were sadness (4.65 out of 7), fear (4.22 out of 7), anxiety (3.9 out of 7), and anger (3.16 out of 7). They gave happiness the lowest score (2.22 out of 7).

Fear, in particular, is being deeply conditioned in us today. We fear not just being controlled but being unseen. We fear that we will leave the earth without having left a mark on it. We don't know exactly how we will fare if we step too far out of line, whether our friends will still talk to us, whether we will be cast out of book club or locked out of our bank account.

If our civilization collapses, it won't be because of an outside attack, like Bedouin charging in from the desert. War or global famine might issue the fatal blow but the real killer will be the parasites that destroy us from within, our excessive pride, the loss of meaning that unmoors us from the past, the incivility that gnaws at the threads that hold us together. It will be because we've lost the plot and, with it, everything that gives meaning to our lives as individuals.

...FINDING MEANING

"What are we? Humans? Animals? Savages?"

So asks the *Lord of the Flies'* Piggy, the philosopher, the one who keeps the signal fire going, the one who remains a passionate believer in civilization.

Aristotle's answer, one that I think would have resonated with Piggy, is that man is "by nature a political animal."[78] It's not that we are particularly interested in politicians or the politicization of issues but in living together with others, in friendship and in humanity. As the William Blake scholar, John Higgs, writes:

> True politics are not ideologies to discuss, but an attitude to your relationship with the world which is enacted in your daily life. Your politics are not what you tell yourself you believe. They are not the set of ideas that you identify with, or look to for personal validation of your goodness as a human being. Your politics are expressed in the choices that you make, the way you treat other people, and the actions you perform. It is here that hypocrisy and vanity

fall away, as the reality of your politics is revealed in the countless decisions that you make every day. Who you work for, whether you volunteer for charity work, if you become a landlord, whether you eat meat, the extent to which you pursue money and consumer goods — these are the types of decisions in which our true politics are expressed…

If we want to live well, then striving for perfection and conformity might just be the worst ways to go about it. Our humanity is made by how we think, how we treat each other, and in all the big and little decisions we make every day. It is made in our own choices and actions, however imperfect they may be by some objective measure.

So how did we get so off course? When and why did we lose our humanity?

Part of the answer is surely the one we get from Matthias Desmet; that our decline began when the Enlightenment took a turn.[79] The Enlightenment ushered us into a modern era defined by a mechanistic ideology, the idea that natural things are just complicated machines, composed of parts governed by physical laws that science alone can understand. This ideology created a utopian vision of a flawless and inevitable future. But we also became atomized, separated from traditions, nature, community and the fruits of our labours.

In a way, the Enlightenment was *too* successful. By focusing on the powers of the intellect, we moved away from wisdom and virtue, and as beings who are able to use these to shape meaningful lives. Reason, as Hume said, remained a "slave of the passions." With our resources singularly focused on supporting technical innovation, we became enslaved to it, unable to do the philosophical work of figuring out why we do what we do. Over time, our obsession with reason became an ossified myth (a metanarrative, in postmodern terms). Though it might seem extreme to say, for the German philosopher Theodor Adorno, the Enlightenment led directly to Auschwitz.

Fast forward to today. Just as it wasn't the tower, itself, that was the problem, our problem is not a development in vaccinology; our problem is the set of ideologies that buttress it, and our dependence on them to give our lives meaning. Today's vaccine confidence signifies a certain class position (elevated, educated, clean, and bourgeois), a certain worldview (scientism), and a certain religion (atheism and Scientific monotheism). Anyone who opposes it, by contrast, are COVID's proletariat. The truckers, in particular, were ripe for being portrayed as low-class, uneducated labourers who are anti-science and, to make matters even worse, Christian. Wrong class, wrong worldview, wrong religion. And so they could not be tolerated.

I spent a long time thinking about why the majority was so quick to latch onto the vaccine story and why so many, even now, are unwilling to let it go in the face of evidence begging us to do so. And I often ask myself, what would vaccine enthusiasts lose if the story turns out to be false?

The truth is, they would lose an awful lot. If it turns out that the technology is ineffective or unsafe, or worse still that there was an intention to be deceptive about it, vaccine enthusiasts suffer not just the embarrassment of misplaced beliefs; they suffer an existential crisis caused by the collapse of the ideologies that led them to support it in the first place. If those beliefs turn out to be suspect, so too is everything else they hold dear.

But all is not lost. On the contrary, this realization actually offers some hope, a way to step out of the quest for immunity and invulnerability, and ask ourselves who we are, why we do what we do, and how to reconnect with the most meaningful parts of our past and ourselves. It is, ultimately, inspiring and deeply human.

Though Ancient Greece and Rome eventually fell, our civilization is built on the foundational ideals that endured long after their physical structures and governments crumbled. Justice, beauty, courage, character, self-knowledge. They endured because we found them meaningful. They endured, and will endure, through literature and art and conversation and ritual. They will endure in how we gather, how we write about one another, how we care for our sick and our aging, and how we envision our future. They will endure if we decide it's more important to be human than to be perfect.

If we are to remain civilized, we need to remember that we are primarily human, that we can use science and technology to craft ourselves in various ways, but we must be vigilant in resisting a 'progressive' decline away from meaning and value. Facts must always be molded by values lest we become enslaved to our own ingenuity.

LESSONS FROM BABEL

What can we learn from Babel that can help us now? If the Babylonians were wrong to build their tower, what were they supposed to be doing? What do you do if you are the one who starts to worry about the project? If you think maybe it has the wrong goals? What could the Babylonians have done that they didn't do? What can we do now?

As a philosopher and a Christian, I think about our problems and their solutions in terms of abstract ideas rooted in who we are as mortal, flawed beings with free will. And this makes a big difference to how optimistic I can feel, and how I think through the options available to us.

I think the Babel story teaches us two key general lessons: one is personal and the other collective. One is a cautionary tale about the natural consequences of failed personal governance, what happens when we let arrogance run roughshod over the more careful steps of our conscience. The other is a warning about the power of humans working together towards any kind of utopian project. We forget that living well is not necessarily a matter of living bigger and faster or across multiple dimensions, but that we can only be useful beyond ourselves if we first give our souls the attention they need.

And, if there can possibly be anything good to come out of the horrors of the last four years, it is this: some of us, at least, have been shaken awake. We now know that we are under attack. We are under attack not so much for the particular things we say or do but simply for wanting to be free, for wanting to be able to think through our lives, which will be the products of our own choices. Below are some specific lessons from Babel that might be able to help us now:

Human nature can't be transformed instantly: At the end of a long battle, when moral resources are in short supply and hope is a scarce commodity, it's easy to grasp at quick and easy solutions. But it will take time, and probably many missteps, to learn the lessons we were supposed to learn on the plains of Shinar.

In the fall of 1993, Aleksandr Solzhenitsyn delivered a speech at the dedication of a memorial to the thousands of Frenchmen who perished during the Vendée genocide in western France. During his speech, Solzhenitsyn warned against the illusion that human nature can be transformed in an instant. He said, "We must be able to improve, patiently, that which we have in any given 'today.'"

We need patience now more than ever. But we need *active* patience, to speak when we are able, to keep a soft heart when it would be easier to harden it, and to water the seeds of humanity we find when it would be simpler to plough them under.

Don't give up on meaning: It's easy to see why so many are tempted by nihilism. I even catch myself wondering, have we passed the point of no return? Can we still pull ourselves back from an abyss of nihilism and mindless collectivism?

In Goethe's *Faust,* Mephistopheles' fundamental motivation is to make us so disenchanted with our humanity that we give up on the project of living. And isn't that the ultimate way to destroy a person? To convince him that all the little choices he makes everyday are futile, and that humanity, itself, is an unwise investment? How do we navigate the hazards of excessive pride, on the one hand, and nihilism, on the other?

The first thing is simply to *decide* that we aren't going to let meaning be stripped from our lives. Our lives mean something and they mean just as much as they did before we were told that they mean nothing. But meaning isn't passive or spontaneous. We need to *give* meaning to things, *see* meaning in things. And we need to keep doing it even when the world refuses to validate our efforts.

A room of one's own: Virginia Woolf once described a woman whose thought had "let its line down into the stream." But, as soon as she started to think of an idea, a man enforced a rule whereby women are not allowed to walk on the grass. Abiding by the rule, the woman loses her idea.

We know too well how everything from social expectations to peer pressure to being nudged can make us abandon our consciences and conform. The antidote, according to Wolf, is to carve out a space where we can hear and create our own thoughts.

Back to *1984* for a minute. In the novel, the reason interactions are monitored so closely is because intimate relationships provide a safe space for ideas. In response to the Party's attempts at control, Julia and Winston form their own little group where they share and nurture each other's ideas.

We, too, need a room of our own where we can dampen the noise of the madding crowd. Once we have this, we can build a little annex for trusted others. We can shut off social media for a while, play an instrument, go for a run, revisit photos from our childhood. Do whatever is necessary to give ourselves some distance. You don't need to absorb everything from the world, you can be morally aware without becoming a moral chameleon.

Humility: One of the great lessons of Babel is what happens when our pride gets out of hand. It "goeth before destruction," Proverbs 16:18 tells us, and is the original and deadliest of the 'seven deadly sins.'

Pride is stubborn. It is thinking we can carry our own burdens, that we can be God. The Ancient Greeks knew pride is futile, a foolish way of investing energy in the humanly impossible.

The opposite — humility — is depending on others. C.S. Lewis says, "Humility is not thinking less of ourselves, but thinking of ourselves less." He says pride gives us the false impression that we can build towers to reach heaven and use science to become invincible. The cure, if Lewis is right, is to realise our place in something greater than ourselves.

Embrace the lack: Today, so many of us feel a lack, an emptiness in the very depths of our being, an emptiness that no number of Amazon purchases, social media 'follows,' or virtue-signalled projects will fill. Not for long, anyway.

It is natural to think that we have this lack because of something we are missing. We think we would be better off with a different Prime Minister, more financial stability, or better friends. We think something eludes us and so we set out to find it.

But what if our problem is not that we lack anything but that we have too much? Too much that distracts us from what really counts. What if we feel a lack only because we abandoned ourselves for a while? Like when you are away from home for too long and forget about all the little things that ground you. What if we've just lost the perspective to see that we already have within us all the resources we need to live better: the capacity for self-reflection, a conscience, and the ability to develop and maintain personal integrity? If the Babylonians had these, they might not have built a tower. If we had them now, we might be less obsessed with inventing problems so we can find meaning in their cures.

Fragility and control: It's easy to respond to the feeling that we are losing control by tightening our grip on what we can control. So we let our technical prowess create a false impression of invincibility. If we can fly to the moon, why not to Mars? If medicine can make us live longer, why not forever?

But, at every turn, we are reminded that trying to control the world around us is a 'fool's errand,' and that there is beauty in the fragility and chaos of life if we choose to see it. Perhaps the worst thing we can do in this moment is to give up on life and on each other. It's tempting to do so and to back away from a culture that is letting you down. This is a temptation I need to fight hard, often being too quick to turn from people that disappoint. But that is a double-edged sword; though it offers feelings of relief and security in the moment, it means losing out on something much more meaningful.

The Babylonians got it wrong by aiming for something outside themselves. They tried for transcendence and destroyed themselves in the process. They were supposed to spread out over the earth, a very messy and mortal project. Instead, they decided to unite and build upward. Human meaning isn't to be found in trying to rise above our fragility but, rather, in sinking into it, and making ourselves ever more human by doing so.

CONCLUSION: IT'S HOW YOU WALK THROUGH THE FIRE

Sometimes it takes a good 5,000 years to learn the simplest lessons.

It's hard not to be worried about the state of our civilization today. With a looming financial crisis, the next gain-of-function virus galloping over the horizon, demagoguery, and the growing "IBG/YBG" attitude, it's natural to look for a panacea, the one that will return us to a more innocent world.

But let's be careful what we wish for. If the proverbial genie popped out of the bottle and asked what kind of life you want, what would you say? You could make all your troubles disappear in an instant. You could wish for the simplest solution to our complex problems. You could. But, should you?

If you're reasonable about it, you won't wish for a panacea. Because then you wouldn't know what it is to develop yourself through the process of challenge and trial and self-discovery. In a crisis, it's natural to look for the easiest way out. But it can be too easy to forget that the gift of our trials is not being able to dissolve them but learning how to make ourselves through them.

When he was in prison for reproving Stalin in a letter to a friend, Solzhenitsyn wrote: "Bless you prison, bless you for being in my life. For there, lying upon the rotting prison straw, I came to realize that the object of life is not prosperity as we are made to believe, but the maturity of the human soul."[80]

The maturity of the human soul. Isn't *this* what we should be after, after all?

Pain and uncertainty, though uncomfortable, are not always as bad as they seem. And they certainly aren't avoidable. As Charles Bukowski wrote, "Things get bad for all of us, almost continually, and what we do under the constant stress reveals who/what we are."[81] What matters most, he wrote, is how you walk through the fire.

Personally, I have never done so much grasping, reflecting, questioning, and listening as I have done over the last 3 years. As awful as so much of it has been, what better state is there for a human to be in than that? This is the stuff of soul-making.

The 2nd century theologian Origen said that the world is a "Hospital of Souls," causing pain in order to cure us of a disease (an ancient version of theologian John Hick's 'vale of soul-making'). The worst parts of our world, as regrettable as they are, give us a chance to work on ourselves and to learn from our suffering.

Let's return to Piggy's question: "What are we? Humans? Or animals? Or savages?"

Ironically, it's in trying to become superhuman that we have turned ourselves into savages. Our redemption lies in remembering that, more important even than perfection, is refusing to give up on the sacred concept that is at the core of the dignity of every human life. And if we remember that, we will have gone a long way to reclaiming it.

Conclusion: How Will Our Story End?

We were here; we are human beings; this is how we lived. Let it be known, the earth passed before us. Our details are important. Otherwise, if they are not, we can drop a bomb and it doesn't matter...

—Natalie Goldberg, *Writing Down the Bones: Freeing the Writer Within*

Moments before I sat down to write the conclusion to this book, I had an encounter that shook me. I went into a shop to pick up some paint for a project at the house. Indulgently, perhaps, I looked forward to a moment of escapism, some time to let my right brain play a little in a land of colours, textures, and imagined spaces. I wasn't looking for meaningful conversation. I certainly wasn't expecting confrontation. Before I left, the shopkeeper asked me about my first book. Her body language was inviting, she was genuinely curious to know more. But her coworker immediately bristled, saying, "Well, hindsight is 20/20;" he proceeded to launch a litany of reasons why we shouldn't hate Justin Trudeau (not that I had mentioned politics.) What became undeniable is that, as the conversation moved along, his gaze became sharper, his muscles tensed. I could feel the ire 'oozing' out of him.

Afterwards, I went to lunch, as I had planned to do, to write what you are reading now. I ordered some soup, which I hoped would warm and calm me a little. It didn't work. Even now, hours later, I still feel shaken by what happened.

Our lives are made up of moments, some more memorable than others, some more impactful than others. Sometime in 2020, we had what I have come to think of as our last innocent moment. Our last moment of being unaware of what was to come and how we would hurt each other. Our last moment of understanding what really drives us and what we had done, or allowed to happen, that got us to this place. Our last moment of knowing how everything to come would put us on a new course.

Whatever happened over the last few years, we have been fundamentally changed by it. There's no reclaiming the innocence we lost. Life is more serious now. Our obligations are more weighty, or just more apparent. There are certain truths we came to see that can never be unseen. And everything is so much more complicated than we thought.

One thing COVID showed is that how well a society endures a crisis or rebounds from one says a lot about how strong it was when it entered the crisis. And how we endured COVID is more telling than it might be comfortable to admit.

"Let them die."

The fact that these words were strewn not in orange spray paint on the dirty walls of an overpass but in bold, carefully chosen font on the front page of our country's largest newspaper *and* the fact that they received so little criticism — when that kind of bigotry moves out of the shadows and into the public square — means that it's not about the hated, themselves. It's about those who do the hating. It's about the state of our nation and the cultural forces that festered long and strong enough to gain the momentum they needed to parade, unapologetically, in public spaces. It's a sign of a deep social pathology. It's a symptom of our self-destruction. And it's an explanation for why the most educated and elevated among us responded to these words with savagery rather than civility.

And this is also why, of the many horrible things COVID did to us, it trained us to focus on numbers (though not, in my view, very accurately). But numbers are just symbols, ways we organize a chaotic environment. They represent things about our lives but they are not life itself. An adverse event number is a woman suffering so many strokes that she fears she will wake up and not know who she is, a teenager who takes her life during a third lockdown, a longed-for baby who is "born sleeping." The COVID narrative wants to teach us that we are insignificant, that our voices are silenceable, and that our individual lives are made meaningful only by sacrificing ourselves at the altar of scientism and perfectionism. This is the reality to which our complicity, and our moral blindness, has brought us.

As I approached writing the conclusion to this book, I spent a long time thinking about what I should say about what we invited into our lives by the big and little choices we made over the last four years. I thought about what I could say to offer some hope, a light at the end of the tragic tunnel. Isn't this what we want, after all? A happy ending to our crises? Don't we want to know that it all might have meant something?

But, I wonder, must stories always have happy endings to be good stories? Or can we learn as much or more from the sad endings, the disappointing endings, the ones that leave you wanting to know how it all could have gone so tragically wrong?

As I worked on the essays in this book, my fears mounted about finishing the story with a false promise. To create the illusion that the solution to our problems is easy or that someone might step in to save us.

It isn't. There isn't.

I think it's going to take years, maybe even decades, to work out the tragic flaw that brought us to this point. But we still need to get up each day, put one foot in front of the other and make the best choices with the opportunities and people we have. So I would like to end with a few thoughts going forward, some sweeping and abstract, others a little more practical.

FORESIGHT IS 20/20

As my fingers sat poised to type after my paint shop experience, my thoughts kept returning to the comment "Hindsight is 20/20," as though our COVID mistakes were justified because we simply didn't know better. But we didn't need hindsight; we had *fore*sight. We had all the pieces of the puzzle going into 2020 — about the history of pharmaceutical collusion with government, about how the vaccine industry became captured by politico-economic forces, about how scientism and perfectionism were filtering into our highest institutions, and about how complacency has taken hold in our culture and in our souls.

Everything that should have shown the COVID response to be a massive failure — the Pfizer report, the National Citizens Inquiry (2023) and Public Order Emergency Commission (2022), the breakthrough cases, the displacement of informed consent with Behavioural Insights strategies — failed. Everything that should have quelled our fears — the reality of IFRs,[82] the availability of effective early treatments — only stoked them. The questions that should have been asked *every* day by *every* person weren't asked. Why were pregnant women so willing to experiment on their unborn children? Why did the vaccinated who contracted COVID insist that "it could have been so much worse?" Why did we turn so hostile and hateful? Why didn't basic critical thinking help us? Why did the lesson of failed hubris die in Corinth or on the plains of Shinar or in a German courtroom in 1946? Why do we need to keep learning these lessons time and time again?

So many times over the last four years I heard people say, "I can't wait until the mandates lift," as though that would restore the freedom we lost. But that's not a remedy for the fear that put us here. It's not a therapeutic for the normalization of cancellation and hatred. And it's not a remedy for the complacency that allowed our situation to become rabid and entrenched. None of those things got fixed when the mandates started to lift. None of them have disappeared since. And we shouldn't have expected them to do so.

What the mandates did brilliantly was to create a first-round elimination test, weeding out of our professions and highest institutions the conscientious objectors, the whistleblowers, the critically thoughtful, and the most fearless. By eliminating those who were right to resist, we have homogenized the workforce and, with it, the ways policies will be determined and enforced, how we will receive medical care, how we will be represented in court, and how our children will be educated. How much less likely will it be now for judges, doctors, educators, and politicians to resist when those who proved most able to do so have been eliminated?

Those who challenged the narrative will never be at the top of the fields they once loved; there will be no questioners who make partner, no dissenters who become Chief of Staff, no courageous academics made Full Professor. These are honours reserved now only for the most compliant among us. The mandates, and our submission to them, created a globally compliant workforce waiting patiently, and compliantly, for the next push on our liberty, a push that will only need to be minimal at best.

Sometimes I allow myself to make a wishlist for the future. If I could change the world with a snap of my fingers, what would I wish for?

Some things are pretty clear. We need technology to follow our values rather than create values for us. We need our scientists to cling fearlessly to independence, curiosity, and uncertainty. We need our physicians to rise above their culture of compliance and, as cliché as it sounds, protect their patients *whatever* the costs to their reputation or bank account. We need journalists to report facts, and not feed the narrative spin machine. We need our courts to abandon judicial notice. And, we need individualism to triumph over collectivism, humility over hubris, and as controversial as it may be to say, nationalism over globalism.

Over the last four years, we've seen humanity move quickly and disloyally from one heroic figure to another: Tam and Fauci to Gates, and then Zuckerberg and, even in the freedom camp, from Elon Musk who will 'save the world' by purchasing Twitter, to Danielle Smith or Robert Kennedy, Jr. or some other Olympian political figure who will "bring fire to the people." Without a moral compass to tether our lives, we've become conditioned to outsource our thinking to the current saviour of the moment. But the truth is, there is no politician who will save us, no billionaire who will cure what's really broken in us.

If we are waiting to be rescued, or for those who wronged us to make amends, I fear we will be waiting a very long time. We can wish for grand sweeps of political and cultural change. But, at the end of the day, the only thing we can control are the shifts in ourselves. We need to think better, remember better, vote better. We need to resist when it would be easier to give in, to charge ahead when it means leaving the warm embrace of the crowd. We need to learn how to stand up and say "no," to hold tightly to the mast even as the torrent blows around us.

Yes, we must regain control of our captured institutions but, first and foremost, we must regain control of ourselves.

So where do we start? First, we need to confront the true costs of our compliance. So many kind and thoughtful people I know even to this day defend their compliance. "The grocery store wouldn't let me in without a mask sign so I had to wear one," a young mother of five recently told me. "If I don't comply, I won't be able to help anyone," nurses have said. But this is all 'little picture' stuff. I know how scary it is to stick out one's oar into a tumultuous sea. I can see how it might even feel right in the moment and how good it feels to make a noble concession for the sake of possibly doing something bigger and better.

But, as Hannah Arendt showed us, just 'following orders' will always incur a debt that will be difficult to pay. And getting the engines of autonomy going again, overcoming moral inertia, is a lot harder once its gears have ground to a halt.

Is it enough to resist tyranny in your heart and hope that by doing so you've somehow sidestepped the next atrocity?

Is it enough to talk about loyalty and then shun your noncompliant friend from the coffee circle?

Will courage and integrity suddenly appear the next time your liberty is 'pinched?'

I think it's unlikely. The COVID narrative, and our compliance with it, has created a powerful cultural force that will now be even more difficult to resist.

As a citizen, a student of history and a mother, all of this terrifies me. I'm terrified that the politico-economic forces that wrote the chapters of the COVID crisis will now move into even more intimate zones of our lives and that, next time, it will not be so easy to resist. I'm terrified that those who managed to say "no" the first time around won't have the strength to manage the next crisis as well. I'm terrified that the lessons of history that should have prevented all of this will be permanently shut up in the tombs of our memory. I'm terrified by what we've done and by what this has shown us to be capable of.

But I am also reminded of the Ancient Greek idea that courage isn't the absence of fear; it's finding a way to move through the fear so as not to become paralyzed by it. It's finding a way to let our fears shape us into people who are stronger than we would have been without them. From difficult times come courageous people, it is often said. And quite rightly.

PERFECTLY IMPERFECT

A week before writing this, I sat in the audience at the Eglinton Grand Theatre in Toronto, part of an event on Bill C-47. What I remember most is a metaphor given by Shawn Buckley, President of the Natural Health Products Protection Association and former

Health Canada council. He said that, in any battle, when you are on the defensive, it takes time to organize yourselves. You need to get over the initial shock of having been attacked. You need to figure out what's going on and who the enemy is. You need to buy time, economize forces, and develop conditions favourable for offensive operations. You need to figure out who will do what. And then there is always a point at which the efforts start to take off.

Buckley's metaphor is apt. A war is being waged on us. It's a global and ideologically insidious war, which is as epic and personal as any can be; it's a war not just over personal liberty but over whether our lives mean anything at all.

In fighting this war, there is no single speech or act of government that's going to give us the win. It's a long-term project, with more casualties than we can now imagine. I think our tragic flaw — our scientism and our perfectionism — hasn't yet brought us to our climax and that we are, regrettably, on a course of greater destruction. It's been too easy to distract ourselves, to shift blame, to find places in the sand to bury our heads. Things haven't yet gotten bad enough where it is impossible to do anything else but confront our mistakes.

It is natural to try to improve ourselves through technology — to build better ploughs, taller towers, and more elegant vaccines — and it is natural, in the course of doing so, to cluster against a common enemy. But we get into trouble when the goal of improvement morphs into the goal of perfection. It is in the process of trying to perfect ourselves, to create a utopia, that we ironically and inevitably destroy ourselves. Utopian dreams always become dystopian realities. As Margaret Atwood cautions, "Every utopia — let's just stick with the literary ones — faces the same problem: What do you do with the people who don't fit in?"

We aren't capable of perfection and, ultimately, I don't think we want it. Rather, we want wasted moments and mystery and wonder and raw emotions. We want relationships that expose us to risk. Even unfulfilled dreams have their place in teaching us and making us. Morality is not a self-perfecting game. It takes us out into a messy world full of broken people, a world of fear and commitment and disappointment, and asks us to do the best we can. It requires projects that allow for mistakes. It requires reflection and, above all, humility.

In the process of striving for perfection, and fighting against it, humanity has been trained out of us and, in its place, absolutism, purification and the politicization of all has taken hold. But purification and happiness are not good bedfellows. As the satirist H.L. Mencken once said "Puritanism is the haunting fear that someone, somewhere may be happy." At some point along the way, we lost the joy for life, the lightness to living.

And so the questions we are left with are, how do we manage this problem we keep getting into? How do we develop technology to our benefit, develop the intellect and even make progress, without becoming enslaved to it? How do we navigate the chaos of our world without turning away from it?

Right now, we aren't answering these questions very well. And we aren't winning the war. But we will. The towers will fall and we will build something better in their place. We will win because humanity always cycles through periods of darkness and light, never dwelling for too long in either. We will win because there will always be a small minority, people like you, that hate lies more than loneliness, and whose consciences will always, as Dylan Thomas wrote, "rage against the dying of the light."

THE DEVIL IN THE DETAILS

COVID changed the air that we breathe. Questions that were once treated as complicated inquiries requiring sensitivity and nuance were quickly and efficiently reduced to moral absolutes. Things that so desperately need to be debated — what the science showed, what were the harms for all affected, and what sacrifices we can expect others to make — became irrefutable truths worn as armour we thought we needed to show our purity.

I often ask myself what I have learned over the last four years — about the world, humanity and myself. The thing that stands out is how much harm can be done not just by malice but by ignoring the details. Innocence isn't always pure or childlike; sometimes it can make us a vector for harm we would never imagine ourselves capable of. The paint shop man felt that he now had some hindsight, hindsight that was revealing to him some of the missteps of the last your years, hindsight that was showing him how he and others could have made better choices. But the truth is, he doesn't need hindsight; he could have had decision-informing foresight had he focused on the right details. He didn't and a kind of moral inattention grew in its place.

It's tempting now to try to revise our recent history. We've been through a lot. We're tired, shamed, and traumatized. And we might even be starting to experience the dissonance of seeing what we have done. But we can't fix what we did by forgetting or calling for amnesty. It isn't a coincidence that "amnesty" has the same root as "amnesia:" "men-" (to think). Both involve a failure to think, to pay attention. We have been unthinking. And it cost us.

One of the problems with perfection is that it requires abstraction over digging into the messy details of life. But we aren't supposed to rise above them. The details of our lives are important. As Natalie Goldberg hauntingly writes,

> We were here; we are human beings; this is how we lived. Let it be known, the earth passed before us. Our details are important. Otherwise, if they are not, we can drop a bomb and it doesn't matter...

Our lives are lived in the details, by the big and little choices we make every day. It matters that we remained silent when we should have spoken up. It matters that we thought we could comply our way out of control just as it matters that some of us made eye contact when it would have been easier to look away. The devil may be in the details but so, too, is our truth and our humanity.

This is how we must think, this is how we must treat others, this is how we must frame policy and treat our loved ones as we move forward. If I am right that the situation in which we find ourselves is the natural culmination of our tragic flaw, then like all tragic flaws, it wouldn't be surprising that we are suffering as we try to work it out of ourselves.

Ours is a coming of age story, of sorts, and it's one we are still living. Time will tell whether we fail or have what it takes to learn the lessons we need to learn. Along the way, it can be helpful to remember that, where there's trauma and disaster, there is also opportunity for growth and rebirth. It won't be as easy to learn our lessons, confront our tragic flaw(s) and do the hard work of figuring out who we can be and want to be.

But just because we need to remake ourselves doesn't mean we won't be able to make something better in its place. Just because we can't see the purpose of it all now doesn't mean there isn't one. Like a tapestry that is a jumble of erratically woven and knotted threads from behind; you need only turn it to the right side to see how it all resolves into beautiful, intentional order.

"VICTORY VERTICALS"

When governments around the world started to impose the mandates, and the global population jumped on board enthusiastically, something more profound was being established in ourselves: human 'progress' aimed at by perfectionism and collectivism rather than a well-established democratic order— a paradigm shift signalling nothing less than the imprisonment of the 21st century mind. A prison created by small, incremental encroachments on our freedom, not forcing us at any point but making it so unappealing to refuse that we give in, thinking, "It's just one little thing," "It won't matter that much." This is a prison from which it will be hard to escape.

COVID created much internal juggling for me, some of which

is hard to reconcile with who I thought I was. In addition to the fears and insecurities, I now find patience and toleration in much shorter supply and, maybe most profoundly, I find it hard to enjoy a kind of lightness of being. My thoughts so often feel heavy, bitter, even foreboding. In the height of the crisis, in particular, I often found myself kicking into high-gear strategic mode, and, in the process, I lost a sense of joy about life, something I especially regret in the first months of being a mother.

During World War II, the famed piano maker Steinway and Sons produced specially-built pianos for the American troops overseas. Called "Victory Verticals," or G.I. Steinways, the pianos were purchased by the U.S. Armed Forces for $486 each and airdropped onto battlefields.

When I heard this story, I wondered, why did the U.S. government spend so much money and effort on pianos, of all things, at a time when the materials to make a piano — iron, copper, brass — were so badly needed for other things.[83] Not to mention what it would cost to airdrop a piano over a battlefield in 1943!

They did it to boost troop morale, because they knew the joy it brought, emblematic of that iconic movie scene of Bing Crosby singing "White Christmas" to the troops on Christmas Eve. Even in times of the most profound crisis and instability, we need moments of joy to brighten our heavy hearts.

In a soul-lightening interview with Trish Wood in 2023, Brownstone Institute founder Jeffrey Tucker talks about the importance of joy in times of crisis. He urges us to remember that, while we're working on solving the problems of the world, we must remember to live our lives, to allow our children a peaceful childhood, and ourselves time for things that bring us joy. Look up at the tree canopy, listen to a piece of music without simultaneously scrolling, read for pleasure. If you spend all your time strategizing and organizing the troops, it can be hard to notice the beauty of the land on which you are fighting. In crisis mode, it's tempting to chart a sort of efficiency to your days but it's important to remember that it's in times of crisis that we need these things most.

These days, whenever I fall back into strategic mode, I try to force myself to remember that days are better when I pause to notice the sky, when I read, when I let my mind wander to the possibility of painting again. I force myself to remember that it's in holding onto the joys in life, refusing to collapse under the weight of our fears and insecurities, that we find our humanity. We can't control everything but we can decide not to let dignity be stripped from our lives. And it's the little decisions we make everyday that allow us to hold onto it.

THE STORIES WE TELL

The thing my daughter asks for more than anything else — more than to go to the playground or to have a certain treat — is "Read me another story, Mama?"

Life is not just a series of events but the perspective we take on those events, the stories we tell ourselves. We need stories. We need them to understand ourselves. We need them to make sense of our shifting identities and experiences, and to see ourselves reflected in others so we know we are not alone in this vast, frenzied world.

Not all stories have happy endings. Sometimes they end badly, tragically or even inconclusively. I think our happy ending is a way off. And I think we won't get it until we learn the hard lessons that we're so stubborn to learn.

Sophocles' *Antigone* offers us an invaluable gift in this respect. Torn between obeying the laws of her country and her conscience, Antigone is forced to consider, would it be better to try to craft a risk-free life by simplifying her projects and narrowing the scope of her commitments? The answer is, probably yes. It's relationships and dreams and goals and grand efforts that put us on life's most perilous cliffs, that most expose us to vulnerability and uncertainty. But life without these is also less human. Our humanity is the price we will pay for the efforts of invincibility. And this is a lesson Sophocles tried to teach us over 2,000 years ago.

In many respects, COVID was the best gift we never would have asked for. It was a litmus test for who we were and what we are capable of (bad and good). It's a gift that's forcing us to think about what really makes for a good life. For me, it's not "doing your part" (if doing your part makes you cruel and unthinking), it's not what The World Economic Forum tells you is needed to save the human race, and it's not AI, guaranteed basic income, or moving into 15-minute cities.

If we are going to win the war waging against us, we need to stop telling the story of salvation through individual sacrifice and homogenizing unification projects. We need to tell a more compelling story, a story that brings us back to our hearts and our homes, and is honest about the fragility of human life. A story about how beauty lives not in perfection but in becoming wise and curious in our thinking, brave and generous in our actions, and patient and observant in all the little moments of our lives. Ironically, at a time when all the political, global, economic forces are pressuring us to live outside of ourselves — to the point where we become morally emaciated versions of our former selves — we are seeing that the *only* way to perfect ourselves, the only way to become truly useful to others, is to live within ourselves first.

o o o

How will our story end?

We don't know. We haven't written it yet.

But as we write it, let's remember that human life is actually quite hard, if you do it right. We can choose to stay silent and book the next all-inclusive getaway but that won't make us face the problems that really ail us.

I'd like to end with a thought experiment, one that I used to do with students in my ethics classes. It might feel a bit grim at first but bear with me. Try, if you can, to imagine what someone might say when they give the eulogy at the end of your life. Your daughter, your brother, your best friend. What will they say about how you lived? Will they say you chose to 'fly under the radar,' never ruffling feathers? Will they say you complied even when you knew it was wrong, that you turned away from the suffering around you? Or will they say that, though your life wasn't easy, and you were often afraid and lonely, you always chose truth in a world of lies? Will they say that you were unwaveringly loyal?

It's hard to know, while in the frenetic process of living, what song we will sing at the end of our days, what the ship of our life will look like as it sails away or what we shall hope for once it is clear that we can never go back.[84] But imagining how you will reflect on the totality of your life can help to inform how you live it now. Each human life lasts for only a few moments in time, a fact that becomes more poignant as we age. And it's incumbent on each of us to decide what to do with the finite number of moments we have.

When you've been through a crisis, you need to spend some time thinking through it, diagnosing what went wrong and what you could have done better. We can ask history to help us find answers to the sources of our weakness. We can look for the roots of the problem outside of ourselves. But we can't linger there too long. Ultimately, we need to get up, put on our shoes, and figure out how to walk through our own ashes.

The questions we need to ask ourselves now are:

- How do you push forward in a post-Covid world?
- What do you do the day after the allies come into Germany, the days after the Berlin Wall falls, the moments after the COVID crisis passes?
- How do we look each other in the eye?
- How do you begin to renavigate relationships and, almost unfathomably, start to trust again?

- How do you come to terms with what you did (and didn't do), with who you were and who you can be?

Though it's hard to feel it sometimes, we have more power than we think. No matter what we've been through, it's still possible for each of us to choose an easy life or a meaningful life.

My question for you is, what will you choose? What will you do the next time your government asks you to betray your conscience, the next time you face social exile? What are you going to do in 2040 or, possibly, in 2024? What if it really does cost you your job this time? Will you go down choosing or rise up refusing?

There might come a time in your life, possibly sooner than later, when these questions will be forced upon you. And whatever you choose will, like a positive feedback system, shape who you will be in the future.

For my time in this life, I choose the meaningful life. It won't be easy. It will wear you and break parts of you that you didn't know existed. You might be bone-tired, embarrassed, raw, and alone. But, if you see where we are headed, then you will also see that it is your *only* option. As Ralph Waldo Emerson said, "The purpose of life is not to be happy. It is to be useful, to be honourable, to be compassionate, to have it make some difference that you have lived and lived well."

So, what can you do today?

Think about how you spend your moments.

Go home, bake your grandmother's recipes with your children and tell them about the old days. Go to coffee with a friend and lean into the tough topics. Apologize for your regrets. Talk to your wife. Bring your family together. Craft a novel. Adopt a goat. Visit an impoverished friend. Build a room of your own, but maybe make a little annex for some trusted friends.

Keep working on yourself and the other stuff will follow. As trite as it sounds, this may be the key to our salvation, or at least to our rebirth.

And if you ever find yourself wishing for an easier life, try to remember:

Your children might be walking a worse path if it weren't for you.

Your best friend or colleague or brother might not be alive were it not for you.

A whole freedom movement has been made stronger because of you.

Please don't ever wish for an easy life, to be normal or, heaven forbid, to be perfect.

The world is not an easy place but it is an infinitely better place because of the big and little choices you make every day.

Appendix

Viral
by Matthew Barber

Gone viral
The whole world's in a spiral
And I don't know if the change will come
From a needle or some pixels or a gun
Gone viral

Tribal
Gone tribal
It's always been about survival
And I hope we're not heading for war
Fighting with our double-edged swords
Gone tribal

I know that we've been here before
But since then we've learned so much more

Oh we may have sharper tools
But we don't always know how to use them
After all we're only human
And they don't come with clear instructions
They may save lives or cause destruction

Viral
Gone viral
Time to reach out to our rivals
'Cause we're gonna have to find a cure
None of us could be that pure

Endnotes

1 An example of this phenomenon was highlighted by Dr. Byram Bridle in "Call Volume for Paramedics Went Down in 2020, Up in 2021-2022."https://viralimmunologist.substack.com/p/call-volume-for-paramedics-went-down?utm_source=substack&utm_medium=email Accessed June 4, 2023.

2 The more technical explanation for this phenomenon is that if the visual field that is under examination (the piece of paper containing the duck-rabbit, for example) contains a familiar object, then memorized knowledge about the object's shape and textural properties can facilitate our recognition of it. (We know that beaks are smooth and rabbit fur is not, for example). Neurobiologically, the visual cortex contains distinct layers that function in a rough hierarchy, each responsible for handling a certain level of complexity. The most basic might process lines at a certain angle, while the neurons in the next layer respond to line density. Interestingly, information isn't just passed up this complexity chain; it also runs down from the neocortex's higher levels to the lower ones. UC San Diego neuroscientist Bradley Voytek says, "For every axon coming from the retina into our thalamus before entering our 'consciousness' in the primary visual cortex, the primary visual cortex sends at least twice as many axons back onto the thalamus to modulate the raw signal." This is significant because it means that we are not only seeing what is actually before us; we are also seeing what our brain is telling us is there. It's not that we passively perceive the world *or* that we impose our assumptions on it but rather that our experience of the world is a hybrid reality of raw data presented to our brain and perception through assumptions about what we expect to see. https://www.theatlantic.com/technology/archive/2014/05/10-things-you-cant-unsee-and-what-that-says-about-your-brain/361335/#three. Accessed November 15, 2023.

3 "Non-pharmaceutical public health measures for mitigating the risk and impact of epidemic and pandemic influenza. https://apps.who.int/iris/bitstream/handle/10665/329438/9789241516839-eng.pdf Accessed September 10, 2023.

4 Bardosh, K., Krug, A., Jamrozik, E., Lemmens, T., Keshavjee, S., Prasad, V., ... & Høeg, T. B. "COVID-19 Vaccine Boosters for Young Adults: A Risk-Benefit Assessment and Five Ethical Arguments against Mandates at Universities" in *Journal of Medical Ethics*. Published Online First: 30 Mar 2023. doi: 10.1136/jme-2022-108852

5 Woolf, Steven, Elizabeth Wolf, and Frederick Rivara. "The New Crisis of Increasing All-Cause Mortality in US Children and Adolescents" in the *Journal of the American Medical Association*. 2023;329(12):975-976. doi:10.1001/jama.2023.3517. Notably, all-cause mortality was not significantly impacted in 2020, when the supposedly "deadly" SARS-CoV-2 ran through the global population.

6 https://www.pfizer.com/about/purpose

7 https://unherd.com/thepost/
neil-ferguson-interview-china-changed-what-was-possible/

8 O'Neill, Onora. "Some limits of informed consent" in *Journal of Medical Ethics*. 2003. 29:4-7.

9 *President's Commission for the Study of Ethical Problems in Medicine and Biomedical and Behavioural Research*. U S Code Annot U S. 1982; Title 42 Sect. PMID: 12041401.

10 The Canadian Medical Protective Association, for example, includes these essential conditions for informed consent in its "Consent: A Guide for Canadian Physicians." https://www.cmpa-acpm.ca/en/advice-publications/handbooks/consent-a-guide-for-canadian-physicians#informed%20consent

11 The Nuremberg Code begins "The voluntary consent of the human subject is absolutely essential." Article 1. https://www.nejm.org/doi/full/10.1056/NEJM199711133372006. Accessed November 2, 2023.

12 Article 6. https://en.unesco.org/about-us/legal-affairs/universal-declaration-bioethics-and-human-rights. Accessed November 2, 2023.

13 211 N.Y. 215, 105 N.E. 92, 1914

14 The incidence of narcissistic personality disorder is nearly three times as high for people in their 20s as it is for the generation that is now 65 or older, according to the National Institutes of Health; 58% more college students scored higher on a narcissism scale in 2009 than in 1982. A recent study showed, for example, that 40% of millennials believe they should be promoted every two years, regardless of performance. https://time.com/247/millennials-the-me-me-me-generation/#:~:text=Here%E2%80%99s%20the%20

cold%2C%20hard%20data%3A%20The%20incidence%20of,a%20
narcissism%20scale%20in%202009%20than%20in%201982.
Accessed September 3, 2023.

15 The band, Maroon 5, was one of many that required fans to provide
proof of vaccination or a negative COVID test to attend their shows
in 2021.

16 Plato. *Symposium*. 190b, 191d.

17 Heying, Heather. "Educational Philosophy." https://
naturalselections.substack.com/p/educational-philosophy?utm_
source=%2Fsearch%2Fembracing%2520uncertainty&utm_
medium=reader2. Accessed June 7, 2023.

18 Sagan, Carl. *The Demon-Haunted World: Science as a Candle in the
Dark*

19 As an aside, but one interesting enough to note, Molière's 1668
comedy *L'Avare (The Miser)* takes place as early modern Europeans
were shifting in how they thought about risk and uncertainty. Staged
just as the science and mathematics of probability was emerging in
the work of Pascal, Huygens, and Leibnitz, *L'Avare* embraces the
atmosphere of uncertainty, putting in opposition risk-takers and the
risk-averse. As the characters encounter low life expectancy, usury,
and the risks of maritime travel, they grapple honestly with the
realities of an uncertain world in which assurance (notably from the
French for both certainty and insurance) is sometimes granted by faith,
but is also developed as policy.

20 Plato. *Apology*. 21a.

21 https://shorturl.at/egEGI.

22 ((Owens, Johnson, & Mitchell, 2013; Krumrei-Manusco, Haggard,
LaBouff, & Rowatt, 2019). (Rego et al., 2017; Ou, Waldman, &
Peterson, 2020; Cojuharenco & Karelaia, 2020

23 Lally, Phillippa, Cornelia Van Jaarsveld, Henry Potts and Jane Wardle.
"How habits are formed: Modelling habit formation in the real
world" in *European Journal of Social Psychology*. 40, 998-1009
(2010). Published online 16 July 2009 DOI: 10.1002/ejsp.674

24 This essay is a revised version of "Are We Falling as Rome Did?,"
originally published by the Brownstone Institute, September 23, 2022.
https://brownstone.org/articles/are-we-falling-as-rome-did/. Accessed
October 1, 2023.

25 Laertius, Diogenes. *Lives of the Eminent Philosophers*. https://
penelope.uchicago.edu/Thayer/E/Roman/Texts/Diogenes_Laertius/

Lives_of_the_Eminent_Philosophers/6/Diogenes*.html. Accessed June 4, 2023.

26 Glubb, Sir John. "The Fate of Empires and Search for Survival." http://people.uncw.edu/kozloffm/glubb.pdf. Accessed November 10, 2023.

27 "Pandemic trauma" is a variety of "mass trauma" or "collective trauma," first documented by Kai Ericson in his 1972 book *Everything in Its Path* to refer to the psychological psychological reactions to traumatic events that affects an entire society.

28 Brooks, David. 2020. "How to Survive the Blitz." The Atlantic, March 29. Accessed May 14, 2020. https ://www.theatlantic.com/ideas/archive/2020/03/virus-and-blitz /608965/.

29 Littman, Robert. "The Plague of Athens: Epidemiology and Paleopathology" in *Mount Sinai Journal of Medicine: A Journal of Translational and Personalized Medicine*. 28 September 2009. https://doi.org/10.1002/msj.20137

30 https://psycnet.apa.org/record/2017-57603-001?doi=1

31 https://www.bmj.com/content/344/bmj.e1674.full

32 https://www.ncbi.nlm.nih.gov/pmc/articles/PMC8496947/

33 https://psycnet.apa.org/record/2015-46377-006

34 One of three maxims that was inscribed on the Temple of Apollo at Delphi. Wilkins, Eliza G. (1929). The Delphic Maxims in Literature. University of Chicago Press. p. 1.

35 Maria Popova. https://www.themarginalian.org/2022/06/23/iris-murdoch-the-sea-the-sea/Iris Murdoch. *The Sea, the Sea.* 1978.

36 Emotional catharsis was based on the ancient medical idea that disease is caused by an imbalance or "corruption" of one or more of the humour and the goal of treatment was to rid the body of the excess humour in order to restore balance in the body. Mann, W. N. (1983). G. E. R. Lloyd (ed.). Hippocratic writings. Translated by J Chadwick. Harmondsworth: Penguin. p. 262. ISBN 978-0140444513.

37 Plato, *Republic.* 514a- 516b.

38 After 9/11, more than 80% of respondents shared their emotional experience with others.

Rimé, Bernard; Páez, Darío; Basabe, Nekane; Martínez, Francisco (2009). "Social sharing of emotion, post-traumatic growth, and emotional climate: Follow-up of Spanish citizen's response to the collective trauma of March 11th terrorist attacks in Madrid". European Journal of Social Psychology. 40 (6): 1029–1045. doi:10.1002/ejsp.700. ISSN 1099-0992.

39 I make no assumptions, here, about the true causes of 9/11. My point is

just that, collectively, we experienced it as an emotional trauma.

40 Rimé, Bernard (2009). "Emotion Elicits the Social Sharing of Emotion: Theory and Empirical Review". Emotion Review. 1 (1): 60–85. CiteSeerX 10.1.1.557.1662. doi:10.1177/1754073908097189. ISSN 1754-0739. S2CID 145356375.

41 https://gwern.net/doc/psychology/2006-frattaroli.pdf

42 https://www.bbc.com/future/article/20190218-the-lifespans-of-ancient-civilisations-compared

43 This very old aphorism, which became the more well-known "Time will tell," is typically attributed to *Aeolus*, a fragmented play of Euripides (485-406 BC).

44 https://www.pollara.com/wp-content/uploads/2023/06/Rage-Index-June-2023.pdf#:~:text=June%202023%20Rage%20Index%3A%2049%25%20%28Down%202%20points,to%2051%25%20in%20March%2C%20to%2049%25%20in%20June. Accessed September 5, 2023.

45 Callard, Agnes. "The Philosophy of Anger" in *Boston Review*. https://www.bostonreview.net/forum/agnes-callard-philosophy-anger/ Accessed May 4, 2023.

46 Sasse, J., Halmburger, A., & Baumert, A. (2022). The functions of anger in moral courage—Insights from a behavioral study. *Emotion, 22*(6), 1321–1335. https://doi.org/10.1037/emo0000906

47 Researchers Ben Tappin and Ryan McKay at the University of London found that we are most irrational when it comes to comparing our moral traits to others, strongly believing we are virtuous while regarding the average person as significantly less virtuous than we are. Tappin and McKay. "The Illusion of Moral Superiority" in *Social Psychological and Personality Science*. Volume 8, Issue 6. https://doi.org/10.1177/1948550616673878. Research also shows that we want others to see us as moral paragons. "Impression Management: A Literature Review and Two-Component Model" in *Psychological Bulletin*. 107(1):34-47. http://dx.doi.org/10.1037/0033-2909.107.1.34

48 Plato. *The Republic*. Translated by Allan Bloom. New York: Basic Books, 1968. (351b)

49 Shay, Jonathan. *Achilles in Vietnam: Combat Trauma and the Undoing of Character*. New York: Scribner, 1994, p. 3.

50 Silver, Diane. "Beyond PTSD: Soldiers Have Injured Souls." September 3, 2011. https://truthout.org/articles/beyond-ptsd-soldiers-have-injured-souls/ Accessed November 18, 2023.

51 Walker, Margaret Urban. *Moral Repair: Reconstructing Moral Relations after Wrongdoing*. 2006. New York: Cambridge University Press, 2006. p. 228.

52 Mead, Margaret and James Baldwin. *A Rap on Race*. J. B. Lippincott, 1971. p. 45.

53 Walker, Margaret Urban. "Hope(s) After Genocide." In *Emotions and Mass Atrocity: Philosophical and Theoretical Explorations* by Thomas Brudholm. New York: Cambridge University Press, 2017. p. 214.

54 Angelou, Maya. "That Which Lives After Us" in *Facing Evil: Light at the Core of Darkness*. Edited by Paul Woodruff and Harry A. Wilmer. Open Court Publishing, 1988. p. 22.

55 The original letter, titled "What We Learned from Hating the Unvaccinated," which took a slightly different form, was written by COVID blogger Susan Dunham. https://medium.com/@susandunham/what-we-learned-from-hating-the-unvaccinated-fc428fa0732c Accessed May 3, 2022.

56 https://trishwood.substack.com/p/bearing-witness-is-our-power-against

57 https://www.ushmm.org/learn/holocaust/the-many-legacies-of-elie-wiesel Accessed February 2, 2023. This quotation is thought to come from a speech Wiesel gave at the Legacy of Holocaust Survivors conference at Yad Vashem's Valley of the Communities in April 2002.

58 Brison, Susan J. "Trauma Narratives and the Remaking of the Self" in *Acts of Memory: Cultural Recall in the Present*. Edited by Mike Bal, Jonathan Crewe, and Leo Spitzer. University Press of New England, 1999. Pp. 45-47.

59 Taleb, Nicholas. *The Black Swan: The Impact of the Highly Improbable*. Random House, 2007. The concept, however, dates to a Latin expression from the 2nd century Roman poet Juvenal: "*rara avis in terris nigroque simillima cygno*", 6.165 ("a bird as rare upon the earth as a black swan").Puhvel, Jaan (Summer 1984). "The Origin of Etruscan tusna ("Swan")". The American Journal of Philology. Johns Hopkins University Press. 105 (2): 209–212.The expression became common in 16th century-London to describe impossibility, relying on the Old World presumption that 'all swans must be white,' because all historical records of swans reported that they had white feathers. Taleb, Nassim Nicholas. "Opacity: What We Do Not See." Fooledbyrandomness.com/notebook. htm. Retrieved October 1, 2010.

60 Webb, Allen (December 2008). "Taking improbable events seriously: An interview with the author of *The Black Swan*" (PDF). McKinsey

Quarterly. McKinsey. p. 3. Archived from the original interview on 7 September 2012. Retrieved 23 May 2012.

61 The term "unknown unknowns," was made famous by Donald Rumsfeld at a US Department of Defence news briefing on February 12, 2002. The term also appeared in a 1982 *New Yorker* article on metal fatigue as the cause of crashes in Comet airliners in the 1950s.Newhouse, J. (14 June 1982), "A reporter at large: a sporty game: i-betting the company", The New Yorker, pp. 48–105

62 In 1937, the *New York Times* called lobotomy the new "surgery of the soul" yet the majority of patients were left unable to walk, communicate, or feed themselves, or with an altered personality. By the 1950s, lobotomy was generally considered unsafe. Neurosurgeon Henry Marsh wrote, "It was based on this terribly crude, simplistic view of the brain, that the brain was a simple mechanism, and you could just sort of stick things into it…In reality the brain is utterly complicated and we don't even begin to understand how it all interconnects." The introduction of the Mental Health Act in 1983 made lobotomy and other psychosurgical operations rare.

63 A judge had recently ordered Pfizer and the FDA to publicly release tens of thousands of pages of documentation they had used to assess the safety and efficacy of Pfizer's mRNA COVID vaccine, thanks to a Freedom of Information request submitted by attorney Aaron Siri. https://dailyclout.io/making-history-the-warroom-dailyclout-pfizer-docs-analysis-reports/

64 https://www.wsj.com/articles/the-rise-and-fall-of-a-k-street-renegade-1487001918. Accessed September 6, 2023.

65 Liu, Jessica, Chaim Bell, John Matelski, Allan Detsky, and Peter Cram. "Payments by US pharmaceutical and medical device manufacturers to US medical journal editors: retrospective observational study" in the *British Medical Journal.* 2017. 359. https://www.bmj.com/content/bmj/359/bmj.j4619.full.pdf Accessed June 2, 2022.

66 https://www.scribd.com/document/462319362/A-Doctor-a-Day-Letter-Signed#. Accessed November 2, 2023.

67 https://www.bi.team/wp-content/uploads/2015/07/MINDSPACE.pdf

68 https://www.bi.team/publications/mindspace/

69 Some findings that demonstrate bias have been found in non-human animals as well. For example, loss aversion has been shown in monkeys and hyperbolic discounting has been observed in rats, pigeons, and monkeys.[10]

70 That Nimrod was the one to suggest building the tower is accepted in

many Jewish writings. The ancient historian Josephus states of Nimrod, "He also said he would be revenged on God, if he should have a mind to drown the world again; for that he would build a tower too high for the waters to be able to reach and that he would avenge himself on God for destroying their forefathers." Flavius Josephus. *Antiquities of the Jews*. Translated by William Whiston A.M. Auburn and Buffalo. John E. Beardsley. 1895. 1.113.

71 Ovid. *The Metamorphoses*. Translated by Anthony S. Kline. Edited by Rhonda L. Kelley. 1.151-155. https://ovid.lib.virginia.edu/trans/Ovhome. htm#askline. Accessed November 15, 2003.

72 Kenyon, Kathleen M. *Archaeology in the Holy Land*. 4th ed., Routledge, 1979.

73 Genesis 11:3. Finegan, Jack. *Archaeological History of the Ancient Near East*. Westview, 1979.

74 Sometimes called the "Marburg vaccine," the German biotech company, BioNTech, manufactures the plasmid DNA used to make its COVID-19 vaccine, BNT162, in a plant in Marburg, Germany. https://time. com/5955247/inside-biontech-vaccine-facility/

75 It's worth quoting something Barber said about the lyrics of "Viral:" "Viral is about the accelerated world we live in. A world in which technology grapples with nature and ingenuity spawns unintended consequences. It is a call for humility — a reminder that we don't know everything, and as we edge closer to the gods we must not lose touch with our common humanity." See Appendix for the full lyrics.

76 Orwell, George. *1984*. https://files.libcom.org/files/1984.pdf. pp. 147-148

77 Cerbara, L., G. Ciancimino, M. Crescimbene, F. La Longa, M.R. Parsi, A. Tintori, and R. Palomba. "A nation-wide survey on emotional and psychological impacts of COVID-19 social distancing." *European Review for Medical and Pharmacological Sciences*, vol. 24, no. 12, 2020, https://www.europeanreview.org/wp/wp-content/uploads/7155-7163.pdf. Accessed 15 November 2023.

78 Aristotle. *Aristotle's Politics*. Oxford: Clarendon Press, 1905. 1253a1.

79 Desmet, Matthias. *The Psychology of Totalitarianism*. Chelsea Green Publishing, 2022. Especially pp. 32-36.

80 Solzhenitsyn, Aleksandr I. *The Gulag Archipelago: 1918-1956*. Translated by Thomas P. Whitney. Harper & Rowe, 1973.

81 Bukowski, Charles. *What Matters Most is How Well You Walk Through the Fire*. Ecco Press, 2002.

82 Infection fatality rates.

83 It's notable that, early in the war, Steinway was prohibited from building pianos at all due to a moratorium on iron, copper, brass, and other raw materials. The company used its expertise to build coffins and parts for transport gliders instead until it was granted the contract to make 3000 "Victory Vertical" pianos specifically for troops in battle between 1942 and 1953.https://www.steinway.com/news/features/victory-verticals Accessed November 16, 2023.

84 Inspired by the beautiful wording of the opening lines of Mark Strand's poem "The End" in *The Continuous Life*. Random House, 1990.

Index

Printed in Great Britain
by Amazon